Options Trading

A powerful advanced guide to dominate options trading

by

Jordon Skyes

TABLE OF CONTENTS

Part I

Introduction

Chapter 1: Brief Review of Options Trading

Chapter 2: Advanced Concepts in Options Trading

Chapter 3:Advanced Strategies and Techniques

Chapter 4:Advanced Analysis

Chapter Five:Different Types of Stocks

Conclusion

Part II

Introduction

Chapter 1: Advanced Strategies of Binary Options

Part III

Part IV

INTRODUCTION

What to Expect from Advanced Options Trading

In this book, you will get a recap of the concepts covered in other books. You'll become reacquainted with options trading, what it means and what potential there is in it. You'll also be given the pros and cons, because Options Trading is not for everyone. There are some investors who are better suited for other forms of financial gains. *Advanced Options* will help you to define these risks and rewards and better assess your place in this method of stock growth and domination.

Some of the concepts covered in this book:

What does it mean to understand advanced concepts in Options Trading? How do I apply advanced strategies and techniques? Am I right for Options Trading? Can you invest full time in Options—including pros and cons. What is an advanced analysis and why is it needed? There will be a recap at the end of the book as well to help you retain the information that you've learned, because it's more intense than other books you've received in this series thus far.

Why is it Important to Learn All of This?

You've heard it before; we live in a very global world and it's becoming increasingly so every day. It's important to understand this in order to make money work for you, to manage the stock market and investments. One doesn't even need to ever walk into a bank to save money, to ask for a loan, or to purchase any sort of stock. Everything is wireless, paperless, and cloud-centric. A person who is interested in learning about Options Trading must first get this concept of an intangible money management system before they embark on this study. There can be a sense of free falling if you don't, first, understand the concept of this global environment. And this is not entirely a *feeling* if you don't know what you're doing. In Options Trading, the money you trade up can be one currency and the money you sell off, another. You never hold any of it in your hands. This can be a difficult concept for some people, especially those who are of a more tactile sort of learning mindset. In a sense, you must set this aside and lean on other tools to help you embrace these ideas. Options Trading is most successful for those who have an equal parts logical and instinctual approach. It sounds complicated, but it's not. It's actually quite easy: Accept the "global nature" of the financial world now and attack the process with logic (is this stock already looking funny or is something else making it grow exponentially?) and make decisions based on numbers (how much will I lose/gain by exercising my Call or put now?).

Education is the most important tool a human being can have in any industry, the ability to learn from mistakes and accept new concepts, applying them accordingly. Options Trading is no different. Learn as you read this book. Change what you need to. Make the moves that work for you.

CHAPTER 1: BRIEF REVIEW OF

OPTIONS TRADING

Again, if you haven't read my other two books, I highly recommend that you do so. They are chock full of invaluable information about the *whats, whys,* and *hows* of trading. They are more in-depth than this short recap will be as well, but you can get a basic recap right here.

What is an Option? It's simply a contract that allows the investor to sell off a specific asset, for a predetermined price, before its expiration date. While it's flexible within its contract, it is bound by the rules, and the investor must purchase or sell the option by a certain date, if either one of those actions are going to occur.

Options Trading is a wonderful choice for the investor who is versatile and ready to move with the market. The method, itself, is the most versatile way of acquiring and selling stocks. It allows you to adjust to any situation that arises in the market, which is why it's such an effective method of investment. It can be as careful and risky a situation as you want it to be. For some investors, engaging in the high risk that some options allow for is just what they want. It's where they find their success. For others, it's that ability to be careful and retract investments, when deemed necessary, that appeal *to them*.

One of the most important aspects of this whole method is to know your investment. Understand what it is and what you stand to lose if you make a bad decision, if you don't pull out by the expiration date and end up losing thousands of dollars. Understand how your investment functions; is it even worth your time? Really think about this and learn everything that you can before you dive in headfirst. Be prepared to learn the subtleties of weakness in an option, should they begin to arise. It is this kind of foresight that makes a successful investor. The more practice and education, about Options Trading, you allow yourself, the more adept you will become at this form of investment.

Understand the risks, because they can be great. With Options Trading, you have the opportunity to gain or lose a lot of money. If something seems too risky, reconsider. There will be other times and other Options to consider.

Who is Options Trading NOT For?

Options Trading is not for an investor who wants to handle the stock market in the traditional manner. It's not for the person who wants to invest a bundle of money and assume the entirety of the risk if the market falls.

Options Trading is not for the person who is set on the long haul. Traditional stock traders make their money by waiting out the length of their stock, often for many years, until it offers them some exceptional yields. The problem here is when the stock never goes up, or it fluctuates so much that the trader is living on a seesaw of anxiety, waiting for the stock to grow. It may never grow, and if you're the kind of investor that wants to wait things out, sit on a stock for a decade or more, then Options Trading is not for you.

In that same vein, Options Trading is not for the person who is uncomfortable with an "insurance policy" for their options. If you're not willing to put up a small amount of money for a higher yield, or a small amount of money for a small loss, then this kind of trading is not for you.

Options Trading definitely speaks to a specific kind of investor, but it is also a wonderful choice for those with very little money. You can even be in great debt, invest a small amount, and get out before things go sour, or gain enough to pay off your debt in a very short amount of time. Options Trading is for the active trader, for the person who likes to move things around quickly and to see results within a fixed amount of time.

Some of these concepts might seem repetitive throughout this book, but repetition ensures that you're learning these tips and strategies. So, don't think of them as repetition. Think of them as building blocks that are adding to your Options Trading "educational" portfolio.

Wrap-Up:

Options Trading is not for people who are looking for traditional stock trading.

Options Trading is not for people who are looking for a long-term investment.

Options Trading works well for people with very little investment capital, or low funds.

Understand your investment—learn about the Option thoroughly before making any moves.

An Option is simply a contract that allows the investor to sell off a specific asset, for a predetermined price, before its expiration date.

While there is a lot of flexibility with Options Trading, there is also an expiration date, and it is very important.

Chapter 2: Advanced

Concepts in Options Trading

Now that we've reviewed some of the basics, it's time to get deeply into Advanced Options. Here are some words that you'll be learning and/or reviewing over the course of this book:

Schaeffer's Investment Research offers some excellent vocabulary for those interested in becoming advanced in the field of Options Trading. These terms come directly from their website, but the examples are mine. You can find some additional information about Options and other forms of trading at their website; if that's something you're also interested in. If anything, researching other investment firms and operations will show you just how convenient and efficient Options Trading is. Sometimes, these websites simply reveal how much more complicated and risky other forms are trading are.

Adjustment. When and issue like a stock dividend or split causes an **adjustment** (change) to an existing option agreement. Example: This happens when you are bit unsure of a stock and you want the flexibility to change the Option (or contract) when you're nearing the expiration date. While most

Options have hard rules, an eager seller is usually willing to work with an eager buyer.

Ask price. The smallest dollar amount a seller would take as a guarantee.

Example: You're reading the stock chart and you see that X, Y, Z stock is selling for $50 a share, but you feel that it's worth $45, and that's what you're offering. The lowest amount that the seller is willing to go with their stock is $50. That would be their Ask Price.

Assignment. Providing written document to an option seller instructing him or her to (if it's a call), move or (if it's a put), acquire the insurance at a designated strike price.

Example: An Assignment happens when the seller is forced to sell their stock at the specified price, even if the market falls. So, if the seller has agreed to sell his/her stock for $50, but it goes up to $60, with an Assignment, they are obligated to sell it at that originally assigned price of $50. The buyer wins.

At-the-money. If the strike price of a call or put option is close to the market charge of the necessary insurance it is considered "at-the-money."

Example: A stock is selling for $50 a share, and it's only worth $50 a share. This is what it means to sell stock At-the-Money.

Automatic exercise. The Options Clearing Corporation (OCC), in support of an option holder will without question, use an ending in-the-money option.

Example: A trader buys a share of a stock for $50 and on expiration Friday it is worth $50.05, the call option will be exercised without the trader having to take any action.

Back-month. Any option series that will expire the farthest date away from the closet end date.

Example: You have Options left over from the last month or you're working on one for the next month.

Bid/ask spread. When the **ask** price is greater or higher than the bid **price**, and you subtract the bid price from the ask price, the amount leftover is known as the **bid-ask spread**.

Example: You're bidding $50 for an Option, and the seller is Asking $60. The difference is $10.

Bid price. The amount a buyer or dealer is willing to pay for an asset.

Example: A seller is Asking $100 for an Option, but you're not willing to go any higher than $75. That $75 is your Bid Price.

Black-Scholes. A method to price options; it takes all of the following into consideration: price of the exercise, price of the stock, the expiration time, the interest rate (risk-free), and a stock return's usual deviation amount.

Example: When all the various angles and percentages of an Option have been calculated and firm decisions are made based upon those calculations.

Exercise. When an option holder has the opportunity, but is not required to sell or buy the asset at a set amount on or before a time schedule in the future time.

Example: To exercise, the asset will be purchased by a call owner, and put owners sell the asset per terms specified in the contract.

Expiration date. In terms of options, it is the third Friday of the month of the contract. It is the month when the contract ends. Example: Your Option expires on October 31st. That's your Expiration Date.

Expiration Friday. It is the end date for options in the U.S., usually the third Friday of the month of the contract. The month the contract ends. If a holiday falls on the same day, it will be the day before (Thursday).

Example: It's the last Friday before an exchange holiday, and your Option is expiring. You'll either gain or lose.

Front-month. In trading it is the month of the contract that has an end date nearest the current date. It is usually within the same month, or the shortest timeframe of a contract that can be bought.

Example: It's the Front-month and you have a collection of Options ready to expire. You're calculating them all, considering your gains and losses.

Greeks. The series of possibilities and prospects (measurements) that need to be considered before buying or selling

Example: Self-explanatory.

Implied volatility. A part of all individual options; it is the amount that is backed out when all other factors (i.e., expiration time, price, interest rates, and strike) are considered to find the price of the option.

Example: If a seller is selling an Option for a stock that's part of an oil company that just had a major leak, its Implied Volatility is high. It probably can't be trusted, so the seller lowers the price of the stock to make it more appealing that it would be it if remained at its pre-spill price.

In-the-money. When the strike price of an option is less than the current market amount of the underlying amount (call option) or more than the market amount of the underlying amount (put option). The option has real (intrinsic) value.

Example: Your Option guarantees that you're going to get this stock for $90 a share, but it goes down in value to $60 a share. You have a Put on it, so you still get it for $90, no matter what the market is doing.

Intrinsic value. The actual value (worth) of a company or asset based on the underlying amount after all parts of the company or asset are considered (i.e., intangible or tangible factors

Example: The In-the-Money amount is $100 a share, but the current price is $50 a share. The difference is the Intrinsic Value or $50.

LEAPS. In terms of options, it is choice for options to have lengthier terms than usual options.

Example: An American way of handling stocks and Options. The Option has a much longer term than usual.

Leverage. To use different financial mechanisms or margins to raise the possible revenue generated from an investment.

Example: An Option!!

Open interest. Is the amount of undelivered options or possible options on a specific day, during a specified time period.

Example: If many investors are seeking Options on a particular stock, there's a strong Open Interest. If hardly any investors are seeking Options on a stock, obviously, there is not a strong Open Interest. So, it's an interest, or lack thereof, in a particular stock.

Out-of-the-money. In terms of options, it is when the strike price of the option is more than the share price of the underlying asset.

Example: When you're Option is costing you more than it's worth.

Rolling out. This means substituting an option that is due to expire with one of equal amount at a later time.

Example: You have an Option on one stock, but for the sake price and expiration date, you trade if for another of equal value. Why would you do this? Because you think this stock is going to go someplace more interesting than its previous counterpart.

Rolling up. When a trader switches greater strike priced options for lower strike price options, it is known as rolling up.

Example: Self-explanatory.

Rolling down. When a trader switches a greater strike priced options for lower strike priced options, it is known as rolling down.

Series. In terms of options, it is a definitive set of puts or calls on the same asset. They will have identical end dates and strike prices.

Example: Self-explanatory.

Strike price. The amount set by the seller of an asset after it has been bid on. It is usually for the sale of an option.

Example: You've made a Strike for a particular amount of money.

Spread. It is the difference between the ask and bid price of an option.

Example: You have an Option for $100 a share on this one stock and $75 for the same stock purchased at a different time.

Time decay. It is the fraction of change in the cost of an option in relation to the time for it to end.

Example: Nothing has been lost or gained on your Option.

Time value. When the funds currently available are worth more than an equal amount at a later time because of what it can possibly earn.

Example: The difference between what you paid for an Option and what's really worth.

Volatility. It is the measure of distribution of revenue for a specific asset.

Example: Self-explanatory

We aren't going to cover all of these terms in this book, because this is just a small, but powerful, eBook that was created to equip you with the beginnings of advanced concepts in Options Trading. But, don't worry; this is one in a series, so all of these terms be covered at some point in the lineup.

Take some time to review these terms, to understand what they mean, before you move on. It's important that when the word "strike" or "stop" is used, you know what I'm talking about here. Terms in Options Trading can be tricky, because they are both similar and very different than terms used in traditional stock trading. They can get even more confusing when the word is the same, but the meanings are completely different. So, review these terms every day when you begin this book or a book this in series. Education will yield you the greatest power in this career. The more you understand about how Options work, the better you will get at flexing that gut muscle, the one that gives you a hunch about whether or not a stock is good or bad. But we'll cover the concept of gut feelings and hunches a little later in the book. For now, educate yourself. Study those terms.

Why Options Trading is Actually Less Risky than Trading in Traditional Stocks:

If you've read anything about Options Trading, you've heard how risky they are. You've heard that you can lose your shirt, lose everything if you don't utilize options with care. This is true, but it's also true that the traditional manner in which stocks are traded offer their own set of risks, and they can actually be just as stark, just as devastating. One only needs to think about the Great Depression or the stock market crash of recent years to realize how quickly traditionally traded stocks can fall straight to the bottom. They can yield great successes as well. So, while Options Trading can be risky, so can traditional trading. That is just something to consider when approaching Options Trading for the first time, and frankly, every time you use this approach to financial gains.

Stock traders can only make money one way; if the stock goes up. They also can short a stock, which means that they offer someone a percentage of the stock they don't yet own. For example, if someone wants McDonald's stock, and it's currently selling at $100 a share, the "shorter" believes that it will go down to a much more affordable price to, maybe, $25 a share. This shorter turns to others, trying to convince them that McDonald's stock is going up to $100 a share (even though they think it's going to go down first). So they sell stock they don't have at $50 to investors. What if the stock never goes down? What if it goes up, because McDonald's comes out with a new burger and it's a hit? The stock goes to $150. The shorter has made a promise and must purchase the McDonald's stock at $150 and collect only $50 from his/her investors. They lose big.

Those who trade in stocks, will purchase several (usually hundreds) of shares at a fixed price. For example, they'll purchase 100 shares of ABC Stock (fictional) at $100. This costs the trader $10,000. The trader can only go one of two ways, up or down with this stock. They're holding on for dear life, hoping that the stock goes up, and that they'll make double, triple, or more, back in yields. But what often happens? The stock trader loses in many cases. If the stock falls by 50% in the morning, which does sometimes happen, they'll lose a lot.

An option trader is utilizing a sort of insurance by placing a Call (a contract between two parties to exchange a stock at a strike price by a fixed date) or a Put (placing insurance and protection against loss). For example, they may have also purchased ABC Stock, but they bought 100 shares for a total of $500 (kind of like a $500 nonrefundable deposit for the total $10,000). The Options Trader has an $80 Put. When the market falls in the morning, the same stock is worth the same lesser amount, the Option Trader has the option of selling their ABC Stock for $80 or walking away at $500 within their contract/strike timeframe.

The option trader has a few more tools than the traditional stock trader. They can make Calls and Puts and they can combine the two to form many more options total. They can buy two Calls and two Puts. They can make money and protect themselves from greater losses as well. There are so many combinations of Calls and Puts that the Options Trader, if smart and paying attention to the markets and treating their Calls and Puts as the insurance they are against losses, can protect their income from failure.

Wrap-Up:

Options Trading is less risky than traditional trading because--

All your money is not tied up in one large stock, but diversified across several and protected by a contract.

You can make money even if the stock falls.

Options are insurance against a personal crash.

Options Traders have more tools than traditional traders with Puts and Calls.

CHAPTER 3:ADVANCED

STRATEGIES AND TECHNIQUES

Some things to know about Calls and Puts:

Calls are used for bullish markets. They are utilized when you assume the option is going up.

Puts are used during a bearish market. They work best when you believe the stock is going lower and you need to protect yourself from a great loss.

It can mean the difference between a $50,000 loss and a $5,000 loss. You're getting out before the story gets even rougher. You can even make money with a Put. Your strike can ensure that you sell a stock at a certain price, which ends up being a higher amount than what the stock is actually worth. The one main rule to this strategy is that the investor never forgets that everything in Options Trading has an expiration date. If you fail to handle your Call or Put within the specified time, everything expires.

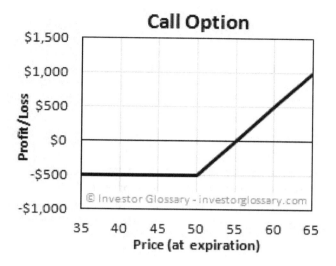

Image of a Call Option in action

(Courtesy, www.investorglossary.com)

Grow A Small Account into Something Bigger:

There are a couple of ways of building your portfolio by using Options Trading. The first one is by purchasing a large number of contracts, maybe 10 to 20, at a low price. This is very important, that the stocks must be low-priced stocks, because Putting an Option on one large stock isn't likely to yield much for you. Variety here is very important. Think of it like this: When a contractor goes to work on a home does he take only a hammer with him? No. He takes an entire toolbox. He might even take several truckloads of tools and other workers to assist him. Why? Because the success of his business depends on the variety of tools he has at the ready. If he only has one great hammer, he can only do one thing at a time. It's the same with Options Trading. If you're going to make a living doing this, or if you're going to grow your portfolio to a size that benefits you financially, you're going to need to Put Options on a large number of low price stocks, in the same way the housing contractor invests in a lot of small tools to make a much bigger business success for himself than one expertly designed hammer can do.

So, what's a low priced stock? Maybe a stock that moves up about $1.00 within a thirty day period. Purchase smaller contracts for those stocks that seem to be moving quickly, but steadily. You don't want to purchase something that has fallen sharply, picked up quickly, and fallen sharply again. Another great analogy for assessing whether or not a stock is a decent one is to think of dieting. Research shows us that those people who diet extremely, who lose more than 10lbs in a week's time, gain it back twice as fast when the diet is over. Stocks can be measured in a similar way. The sudden loss and gain is always something to measure with caution. Did the stock fall sharply in the last 30 days? Is it climbing back up in a measured pattern? Maybe by $1.00 to $3.00 every thirty day period? Then this is probably a stock that's worth taking a look at, and maybe, even Putting an Option on.

Remember, an Option is just a contract. We use Options in all sorts of areas in our everyday lives. We pay a monthly premium on health insurance. Maybe we spend $150-$300 a month on a health insurance plan that covers our check-ups, emergency room visits, and surgeries. Most of the time, nothing serious happens, but does this mean that most people are fine without having health insurance? No way. Why? Because everything could be fine for 25 years of your life. You could, literally, only ever had a cold, but when you fall down the stairs one day and break your arm, you suddenly find yourself needing to make an emergency room visit. Just to get in the door, it's several hundred dollars. The initial nurse triage is another hundred dollars. Then, after hours of waiting, you get into one of the emergency room beds and a new nurse sees you and hooks you up to an IV. Gives you some pain meds. Another doctor comes in to see you. Orders more tests. Now your bill has skyrocketed into the thousands. The person who has health insurance may complain that they have to pay a monthly premium of $300 just to cover one 25-year-old who's never sick, but that complaining ends the day they break their arm and, $10,000 later, they walk out of the emergency room only having to pay the $100 copay.

Exercising the Put Option	Money Out	Money In
An investor buys 1 IBM January 130 Put option for a premium of $9	$900 ($9 * 100)	
The stock price drops to $76, and the investor wants to exercises the Put. He/She must first buy the stock for $76/share. **Cost Basis:** $8,500 ($7600 + $900)	$7,600	
He/She then exercises the Put and sells the stock at the strike price of $130.		$13,000
Once again, the gain is $4,500 **A 53% return on his/her money**		

Sample of exercising the Put Option

(Courtesy, www.learn-stock-options-trading.com)

This is why insurance is so important. It's the same with Options Trading. Why would you throw $10,000 at a stock, watch it crash, and maybe walk away another $20,000 in the hole a month later? This is why Options are important. Yes, they come with risk, but only as much risk as you contract yourself to lose. If you've placed a $100 Put on a Strike, then when that stock falls, you're out only $100 per share, and not, say $500 like someone else.

Another good example of why Options are important when protecting your portfolio is to think of real estate. Say you're looking for a new home and you've been pre-approved for a $300,000 loan. The guy across the street is going to sell his home for exactly $300,000. Awesome. But you're not sure that you want to buy the house for that amount yet. You don't want to be roped into several hundred thousand dollars of debt until you see how other things are selling around the neighbourhood. Maybe, you can end up buying the house for less in the end. So, you offer your neighbor a contract, an Option. You say, "I'll pay $3,000 today, non-refundable, if you promise not to sell this house to anyone else within the next 30 days, and you sell this house to me for $300,000 no matter what else is happening to the housing market in this neighborhood at the end of that time period." You tell your neighbor that this contract binds you to buy this house within 30 days or to walk away having lost $3,000. Your neighbor considers the offer, thinks it makes pretty good sense, and you sign on the dotted line.

This could go one of two ways: In the next thirty days, the house next door to your neighbor's could be sold, without a realtor, to a family member just for the price of the mortgage, and there's only $20,000 left on the mortgage. No profit is made because of this low sale, and it brings down the value of every home on the street. This includes your neighbor's house, which is now only worth $250,000, but if you really love it, and you buy it, you're going to pay $50,000 above market and you'll be throwing much of your money away. So, what do you do? You safely walk away. Yes, you're losing that $3,000 that you saved up all last summer, but you're not stuck in a $300,000 upside down mortgage. Now which one would give you greater heartburn? The upside down mortgage in a neighborhood that's going down in value, or the loss of $3,000 which, if you saved it last summer, you could save it again this summer?

The other thing that could happen in this Options scenario is that the guy's house you're interested in buying could have a windfall. The house next to it could sell to, not a family member but a stranger, and this person could be absolutely in love with the place. She could offer the seller $450,000 just for the gift of living in your neighborhood, and now you can purchase your dream home within that 30 day timeframe for only $300,000. That house has gone up in value now, too, maybe even by $100,000. You can buy that house for a steal, sell it at a much higher price, and make a profit. Options protect your financial future in much the same way that insurance does. So, now that you see how Options are used in everyday life, you can get a better insider understanding of how they work in the financial world as well.

Strategies and Techniques Options Traders Use:

Covered Call. This is also called a buy-write strategy. In this strategy, one would buy assets outright and concurrently write (sell) call options on the assets. It brings in money as a trader gets rid of call options leveraging them against assets already owned.

Reason: Many Options Traders will usually do this when they have a limited interest and really haven't been "wowed" by the asset. They want to make more profits or shield themselves from a possible drop in the asset's worth.

Married Put. In this strategy you would buy (or use owned assets) a specific asset (like a share), and buy a put option for the same number of assets at the same time.

Reason: This is used when traders are bullish on the cost of the asset and want to shield themselves from short-term losses. It functions like insurance and sets a floor in case the asset's worth drops greatly.

Bull Call Spread. In this strategy traders purchase call options at a specified strike price and get rid of the same amount of calls, at an increased rate simultaneously. The call options will have the same basic asset and expiration month.

Reason: A bullish trader will use this strategy when they expect only a slight increase in the price of the asset.

- **Bear Put Spread.** This is a vertical spread strategy where the trader buys put options at a specified strike price and sells the same number of puts at a reduced strike price. Both options will be for the same asset and have the same expiration date.

Reason: Bearish traders use this technique when they are expecting the price of the asset to drop.

- **Protective Collar.** A technique that shields a trader from losing money, and allows him or her to benefit from the rising market and generate revenue without spending a heap of money.

Reason: Traders will use this strategy when a long position in a stock has shown large gains. When doing this, traders can cement a profit without having to sell the shares.

- **Long Straddle.** In this strategy a trader buys a call and put option with identical strike prices, expiration dates, and underlying assets at the same time.

Reason: Traders use this strategy when they feel the price of the underlying asset is due to make a huge move, however, they are not quite sure which direction it will move in. By doing this, traders can receive unlimited gains, while the losses are restricted to the cost of both options contracts.

Long Strangle. Here the trader buys a call and put option with identical maturity dates and underlying assets, but the strike prices are different. It is an evenhanded technique in which the buying of the call and put options are done at the same time.

Reason: A trader using this technique feels the underlying asset price will make a huge move, but isn't sure which way it will move. Any losses are restricted to the costs of both options. Strangles usually cost less than straddles because the options are bought out-of-the-money.

- **Butterfly Spread.** This is another evenhanded technique that has a bull spread and a bear spread working together. It generates small amount of revenue for its low risk. Constructed of calls or puts, three strike prices are used.

Reason: A trader will use this technique when they expect non-spectacular results, or expect the prices to change only a small amount over the life of the options.

- **Iron Condor.** This technique uses four separate strike prices on four separate option agreements. This is a complex technique that takes time to learn about and to master.

Reason: This technique is used when you can get something in return (usually credit) for the sale.

Iron Butterfly. This technique uses four options with three sequentially increasing strike prices. It is like a butterfly spread, but it uses both calls and puts instead of one or the other.

Reason: Traders will often use this out-of-the-money technique to cut their cost and restrict their liabilities.

Wrap-Up:

Calls are used for a bullish market.

A bullish market means you think stocks are going up.

Puts are used for a bearish market.

A bearish market means you think the stock is going to fall.

You can grow a small account to a larger one by utilizing Puts and Calls.

There are several strategies and techniques Options Traders use.

Chapter 4: Advanced

Analysis

Sample Google Stock Chart

(Courtesy, Yahoo.com)

Learn to Read Stock Charts:

Embarking on anything of value requires some education. The more you learn, the more you know, and the better equipped you are at making good decisions that will enhance, and not harm, your portfolio. So, learn to read a stock chart. Learn to recognize when a stock has made a positive trend over the course of its life so far, and when it has been shaky or is moving on a quick or slow downward spiral.

The sample chart above shows how Google stock has performed since it started in 2004. It indicates how the stock started out and how it grew at a steady rate until the year 2008, then it dropped slightly. Remember, just a few paragraphs up, we talked about avoiding those stocks that move up or down sharply, and without a steady progression? Avoid the ones that steadily move downward as well. This seems like common sense, but some people are only drawn to one moment in the life of a stock. They might only see what is in front of their eyes on the Bloomberg Report and not really take the time to study the stock itself. That's where stock charts come in, and this is where they can really assist you in seeing the bigger picture. Charts that show end dates, prices of stocks, and available options are helpful in seeing what can be coming down the pike. You should take the time to study as there is a great deal of data compressed into the chart. Many experts believe it is possible to predict the direction a stock will move in according to its history. This process is called technical analysis and it has been the focal point of many discussions debating whether or not analyzing stock in this manner actually works. Technical analysis says that one can observe past stock patterns, factor in human behavior, and foresee how a stock will perform.

One aspect of technical analysis states that stock has a "level of support," which is the price that a stock won't drop below and a "level of resistance," a price that a stock isn't able to breakthrough. Usually, this will be the case until some phenomenal and exciting news is released and drives the stock above the resistance or under the support, resulting in a change in the lines. See the example chart below:

Sample Google Stock Chart

(Courtesy, Yahoo.com)

In this chart, line A depicts Google's first level of resistance. At the start in 2004, Google had a difficult time breaking through the line right through April 2005. The stock kept delivering great growth and finally broke the resistance line (A) and moved to another phase of resistance line (B), where it remained until November 2005. More great numbers forced that line to break and soon line B became Google's level of support. The level of resistance now seems to be line C.

It seems easy enough to understand, doesn't it? When you look at this chart you can see how some people were able to make money. Once you are able to find the level of resistance, you can buy the stock and when it passes over the level of resistance, you will make money.

Do you understand now? If yes, before you run out and buy a boatload of stock, what happens when additional factors come into play? Not sure what I'm talking about, look at the same chart from above with an additional factor:

Sample Google Stock Chart

(Courtesy, Yahoo.com)

In this example, there is now a line D, which represents the level of resistance up to October 2007 at which time it bursts through the level of resistance. You are tickled pink and decide to buy, buy, and buy. Woo Hoo! You know you're going to be making money hand over fist in no time. But then, the bottom falls out, the stock falls below the level of resistance. It hangs out there for a while, and then drops even more. You're queasy just thinking about it. So what happened? The economic crisis of 2008 caused the drop in price. This shows an issue with technical analysis; drastic changes can make an analysis fall apart.

Look for stocks that jump high, very fast, after a big sell off, but that stay at that steady upward progression. That sell off tells us something about the value of the stock. The owners of the shares have decided that this stock might be worth getting out there in smaller parts. Think of the construction worker mentioned in the example above. Maybe his business has taken a slow turn, and he needs to get rid of some of the tools in his toolbox. He sells off a truck and all that goes with it. He still has two other trucks, but he sells that one truck and all its tools, in part. He makes more money selling parts than he does the whole, and he starts to see his bank account go into the black again. Shares work in a similar way. If you only looked at the contractor's two trucks, versus the three trucks he used to have, you might say, "Well, that guy's not doing so well anymore," but really he is, because he sold off the one truck that wasn't making him a lot of money and each little tool and the truck itself made him a nice profit. He paid his debts this quarter. He's doing well. Look for the stocks that are doing this as well.

This is where reading a stock chart comes into play. You want to look for the Bid that someone is willing to pay for an Option, per contract in other words. Then you want to look and see what the owner of the stock is willing to sell that Option for. These are going to be two different prices. The Bid is going to be lower, because that's the desired price of purchase, and the Ask (the selling price) is going to be higher, because that person is going to want to make some sort of profit, even on the Option (or contract). The Last price is the price that the Option actually sold for. So, what should you actually pay? Add the intrinsic value to the time value and you'll come up with a pretty good price of purchase, something fair you can work with. So, learn to read a stock chart. This will be a tremendous help to you.

With an understanding of how stock charts work, you can better decide when to combine Puts and Calls, when to offer two Calls and one Put. You'll begin to find your way around the Options Trading world and you will become an expert within a short amount of time.

StkExp	P/C	Vol	Bid	Ask	OpInt
360networks (TSX)					20.15
20 Feb	C	3	1.00	1.25	26
22 Mar	C	10	1.60	1.85	138
24 Mar	C	2	1.05	1.25	366
18 June	P	2	2.50	2.75	11
20 June	C	12	4.05	4.30	83
24 June	C	1	2.65	2.90	77
Total option vol. 50			Total open int. 7,492		

Sample Options Chart. Note the Asks vs. Bids.

(Courtesy, Stocktrader.com)

Something About Gut Feelings and Education:

So, what are the most important aspects about dominating stocks through Options Trading? Learn the terms well. We've already covered this. Learn what all the terms mean and how to use the various movements within Options Trading, and educate yourself. The more you educate yourself, the better you'll train that part of your brain that gives you solid hunches and good gut feelings. What do I mean by that? Pay close attention to this section, and re-read it as often as you think you need to.

Neuroscientists have long known that what we call "gut feelings" or intuition is really just the deeper parts of our brains, the more developed parts of our brains that have been working and analyzing since infancy. These are the parts of our brains that help develop a good golf swing and allow us to drive to the same place every day without really thinking about what we're doing. We want to rely on this part of our brain to help us choose what stocks to place Options on. Why? Because it's the subconscious level that picks up warnings and benefits before our naked eye can see them. For this reason, to dominate the market around you in order to build up your portfolio and support your financial life, it's important to train this part of the brain to look for decent stocks, for winning stocks. How do you do that? Practice.

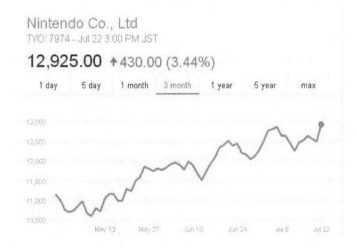

Note how Nintendo's stock, while moving up and down, has a steady

upward progression? This is what you need to look for in a stock.

(Courtesy, Gamenesia.com)

So, learn what you can about Options Trading. Look at the numbers. What is selling steadily? Place a bid here. What is selling erratically? Walk away from that stock. Don't even consider placing any sort of Call or Put. Just leave it alone. That stock can't control itself. You can't trust its consistency. This is something that Options Trading experts have noted for years now, that when you stand back and observe a stock over time, you will see whether or not it's likely to continue in a slow upward trend. That's what you want to look for, the slow upward trends.

There was a scientist in Germany, Gerd Gigerenzer, who did a research project several years ago. He stopped people on the street, making sure that they were completely ignorant of the stock market, and he asked them to choose 60 random stocks they thought would do well over the next thirty days. He worked with several hundred participants, over several months, stopping people on the street and asking them what they knew about stocks (next to nothing at all) and which names stood out to them, which ones they would choose. Once the scientist figured he had assembled enough participants, he put together a portfolio based solely on these random people's gut feelings. He then compared his portfolio to those of very experienced financial advisors. His portfolio outperformed all of theirs by about 85%.

The other financial advisors and his fellow scientists were shocked by this discovery. How could this possibly be? Well, those random strangers didn't stop to analyze indefinitely. They noted which stocks had performed steadily well. They went with names and businesses they recognized.

So, when you're looking for which stocks to choose, don't ponder it too much. Just look at the trajectory of the stock over the past 30 days. What has it been doing? How has it been moving? Is it diving or skyrocketing, or is it, better yet, moving at a steady $1 to $3 gain each month? This is the stock you want. So, go with your gut, with your intuition even more than you go with hours and months of research. Remember that Options Trading is not like traditional forms of stock investment and selling. It is a much faster version of all of that, and it is insurance against great losses. So, while you do stand to lose a lot of money in Options if you Put down a very high bid or strike, there's never any reason to do that. Options are set in place in order to save you from yourself. So, when you're tempted to Put down $10,000 on a stock, because it's moving upwards so fast, think again. Step back. Ask yourself what's so great about this stock? Has it performed reliably in the last 30 days? No. Then you should walk away and not look back. A study done at Johns Hopkins Carey Business School discusses how one should use a decision tree to make sure you consider all options before buying a stock. The questions you place on the decision tree need to cover all possible outcomes on whether or not it will be a good investment.

Here's a sample decision tree, offered by www.sfs.uni-tuebingen.de. This one is for working out the issues of a broken television set, but this method can be applied to stocks as well:

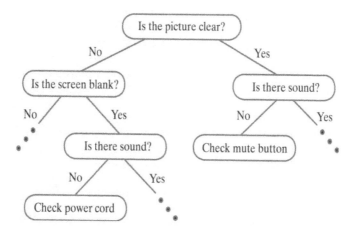

(Courtesy, www.sfs.uni-tuebingen.de)

But if it seems to be steadily moving upwards in the last month or so, Put an Option on it. Put down $1,000 for the next thirty days. Gain even if the numbers begin to go down, because you have a Put on it. You can walk away at a very specific price, no matter what the market is doing. And like Jason Brown of the Brown Report says, "A stop cannot protect you like an Option can" (BrownReport).

For those unfamiliar with a Stop, a Stop can halt the progression of a stock for you, but they're only available to the stock owner during daytime trading hours. So, if a stock falls overnight, there is nothing a Stop can do to protect the investor. A Put can, indeed, protect your investment, however, so this is another reason why Options Trading is the safer exercise on which to embark when you're looking towards buying shares. Remember, how we learned that Options Trading is insurance? Well, this is another example of how it really is. A person who's invested in a large stock, or at least, what is large for them, and then Puts a Stop on the stock during the day, can sometimes save themselves. This is not so during the night when they're asleep. This is something to remember when dealing with Options.

Wrap-Up:

Learn to read stock charts.

Trust your gut feelings.

Educate yourself so that your gut feelings so that are well-informed.

CHAPTER FIVE: DIFFERENT

TYPES OF STOCKS

There are two different types of stocks. Common stock is just what it sounds like, it's common. Common stock equates to ownership in a company and an interest (dividend) on a part of the company's profits. Most stock is issued in common form. Stockholders get one vote per share to select the board members that monitor the staff that will make decisions on behalf of the company. '

Long term, common stocks bring in higher returns than any other investment type. The higher return also means greater risk. If by chance the company goes bust, and has to file bankruptcy and the company is liquidated; common stockholders don't receive any money until all creditors, bond and preferred shareholders receive their cut.

Preferred stock has a limited amount of ownership in a company, but it doesn't have the same rights to vote that common stockholders have. In most cases, preferred stockholders are assured of the same dividend amount forever; a major difference from common stocks which receive varied dividends that are never guaranteed. If a company with preferred stock has to liquidate, all debts are paid first, and then preferred stock holders. Any common stock holders are paid last. Companies with preferred stock also have the ability to buy the stocks (callable) from stockholders anytime and for any reason (in most instances for a premium).

Different Classes of Stock

Although common and preferred are the two main types of stocks, some companies will tailor different types of stocks to suit their needs. Why do they do this? The answer is simple; some companies would like the voting potential to stay with a certain type of group. As a result, various types of stocks are given varying voting rights. An example of this would be one class of stock is held by a preferred group of stockholders (say 10 votes per share), while the bulk of stockholders are given other voting rights (say 1 vote per share).

These classes of stocks are usually named as Class A and Class B to differentiate between the two; like in the case of Berkshire Hathaway (ticker: BRK). Their two stock classes are indicated by inserting a letter after the ticker symbol, (i.e., BRK.A and BRK.B).

How to Determine Good and Bad Stock Investments

The hardest part about investing in stocks is deciding which ones are good investments and which ones are poor choices. There are numerous places to gather information about stocks and it is often hard to determine which source has the most accurate and helpful tips. If you decide to skip using various information sources and make your own decisions, what should you be looking for?

Many news sources show how the stock market is performing by using the colors red and green. While watching the news you may hear something like "the market is down 75 points today," or "the index closed 80 points higher." In most cases they will have some type of chart or graph to accompany the story. For example, if the market goes up, the numbers are shown in green, and when the market drops, those numbers are shown in red. Most sources illustrate financial and money related information in green and red.

Still confused? Think of it in terms of traffic signals. Red lights mean you need to stop and green lights give you the all clear to proceed. Even though stocks are depicted by red and green, that is not the only information you need to consider. Many people have made the mistake of buying heaps of stocks that are shown in green (thinking they will make huge sums of money), only to be let down and lose their shirts. And others may choose to ignore stocks shown in red, to find out later they missed out on a great deal (and big returns) because they decided against buying it.

In order to decide whether or not to buy stocks, you need to look at the complete picture, which includes what you are hoping to gain from buying stock. Do you just want to buy stock and hope the value rises? Are you looking for an investment that will give you annual dividends each year? You first need to decide what it is specifically you are hoping to accomplish, and then proceed from there.

Things to Look at Before Buying Stock

There are a few things you should consider prior to purchasing or investing in stock. They include:

1. **Profit to Earnings Ratio.** Also called P/E, this number tells you how much money you will be paying for every $1 in company earnings.

Example: A stock with a P/E of $15 means that anyone purchasing the stock is willing to pay $15 for every dollar in company earnings. The greater the number, the more it shows that investors are hoping the stock will grow in the future. Usually technology and internet companies have higher P/E's since stock purchasers are hoping for large returns later on down the line.

P/E ratios change so make sure you closely watch the ratio, especially after the earnings reports come out. This will help you determine if the stock is one that you would like to acquire.

2. **Stock Price.** The price of a stock can tell you a lot about it and whether or not the company is a good investment. You need to look at the price history of the stock. There is no stock that rises only and never falls. Check to see how the stock has done over an extended period of time; not just what it is doing currently. See sample Google chart below.

(Courtesy, Google.com)

3. **News.** News is the one thing that you can't easily determine if and how it affects stocks until it happens. Rumors in the news about a company can cause stock prices to rise or fall or no news at all may have a major effect on stock prices. If you are considering buying any stock, you should check to see what the news has to say about it. The news can help you to avoid any upcoming surprises or red flags about the company.

What's Good About Investing in Stocks?

There are many good and bad aspects about putting your money in stocks. If you are thinking about investing, it should be done after doing thorough research to determine how you should go about it. As you are pondering taking a leap into the market, you consider the following:

Opportunity to make money on your investment. When you invest in the market, you can do pretty well for yourself and have some money to save for a rainy day. A stock prices rise, you will start making money to stash in your account. Once you learn how the market works, the possibility is endless as to how much additional income you can generate.

Liquidity. Stocks have amazing liquidating capabilities. When it comes to moving stocks, you can get in and get out without breaking a sweat. No waiting periods. After you make your decision, take the necessary steps to complete the transaction.

Many stocks pay dividends. A lot of stocks like those on the New York Stock Exchange or the American Exchange pay dividends to their stockholders. Earning dividends is like having your own personal quarterly windfall.

Small commissions. Real estate and annuities require you to pay a commission to buy them. One can acquire stocks for as little as a few dollars. With online broker fees under $10, you can sell large quantities of stock for a small amount.

The Difficulty of Investing in Stocks?

Investing in the stock market is not all sunshine and puppies. Sometimes the pendulum swings your way and you make a nice chunk of change. But if it doesn't swing your way, there could be some money slipping through your fingers

Timing is important. Stocks can be fickle, delicate, and mysterious. If you don't fully understand how the market works, your money can fly right out the window. CD and real estate investments don't usually generate large losses. Stocks on the other hand, when they fall, can create staggering losses that can reach thousands of dollars

Stocks sometimes won't rebound for extended periods of time. When your stocks lose their worth, there could be a lengthy wait until it starts bringing in some cash. Some companies will never rebound from the fiasco and have to file bankruptcy and fade away. If this happens, investors may not be able to receive any relief.

Any type of news can sink your investment. A lot of companies play their cards close to their vest. Some will just shock and surprise their investors; leaving investors in limbo before dropping some dastardly news. When the news hits, there may be no time to dig yourself out or jump ship.

Your fate is often in the hands of company management and the market.

A company with a stellar outlook and a steadily growing earnings report can experience a setback. Stock worth could fall when this happens. Steadily growing stocks can burn out and fall just as quick as they rise.

Many stocks have no value. Solid companies are susceptible to the same outside influences as new companies. Some companies have what it takes to flourish and grow in an ever-changing market and others cannot.

Possibility for losing big. If you decide to invest in the market you should always remember there is a chance that you can be successful, unsuccessful, or in some cases remain in the same position as before. Losses are unavoidable and you can lose everything if you are not careful.

Wrap-Up:

- Common and preferred are the two stock types.

- There are different types and variations of stocks.

- Important things to consider before buying stock.

- As with any other investment, there will be positive and negative points to think about before buying stock.

There is much to consider before purchasing stocks or taking part in Options Trading. Of course, you should examine your own personal finances to see if Options Trading fits into your budget.

Like with anything else, you should take the time to do some research to find out if Options Trading and investing is an appropriate action to take. One has to be willing to learn how to properly buy and sell before seeing any windfalls from investing.

Familiarize yourself with all the terms used in trading and buying and selling stocks and study how to apply them to your holdings. Learn the ways and means Options Traders use and see which situations they apply to and give them a try. Being a successful Options Trader will be based on your willingness to take your time and research and never make any purchases blindly.

Options Trading is considered less risky than working with traditional stocks. In the case of stocks, you will only make money when the price of your stock rises. Options traders have more options and ways to make money and they can implement different strategies and techniques to ensure their investment meets their demands. The best way to determine which will work better for you is to try them all and document your results.

It is important to learn how to read stock charts so you are not flying by the seat of your pants or blindly guessing. Review different types of stock charts and you need familiarize yourself with all of them so you can make informed decisions. Read, study, and read some more. This is your money, your future. Do you want to go through life guessing and taking the advice of strangers?

Take the time to seek out as much information as you can to make any type of decision that will affect your financial future. Research stocks and options like you research buying a car. You need to consider every possible option and it may even be helpful for you to do a couple of practice runs prior to investing actual money. What I mean by this is, pick out a few options you are interested in and research them. Study their growth over an extended period of time, read all the information you can find on them, listen to news reports, and study their annual reports.

Once you feel you have gathered enough information to make an informed decision, start off small. Avoid investing huge sums of money in one option or stock or taking advice from anyone willing to share their thoughts with you. You wouldn't seek medical advice from someone riding next to you on the subway would you? So why would you take financial advice from them either.

Whenever you are in doubt about how to handle a specific situation, go back and review the chapters in this book to better help you make an informed decision. Study the market, learn how to read the charts and you should be able to make wise, informed decisions.

Read, absorb, and read some more. You can never do too much studying when it comes to your financial future. If you follow the tips and techniques in this eBook, you will have a good foundation for building a solid Options Trading career. It's your future, do everything you can to make the right decisions on your financial future.

CONCLUSION

I hope that you have enjoyed reading through this book, and I hope that I have been able to assist you in understanding Options Trading, and all its terminology and processes, a little better than you understood it before you began reading. I hope that I have shown you the pros and cons of engaging in this kind of trading. And I hope that you are walking away from this book with a large measure of confidence about what you can, and cannot, expect from a part-time foray into Options. Even more importantly, I hope that if you're looking to make a fulltime career of Options Trading, that I have assisted you in making some very important decisions and learning something you didn't know before. Again, if this is the first book of mine you have read, I highly suggest you read the other two-- *Options Trading: Powerful Beginners Guide to Dominate Stocks* and *Options Trading Strategies to Dominate Stocks*. Like this book, they're concise and consistent books that are chocked full of information to help you learn more about this exciting world of Options Trading. This is a series, so expect more!

Jordon Sykes

ADVANCED GUIDE

To Dominate Binary Options

INTRODUCTION

What are Binary Options?

Known by various other names such as "Digital Options" or "All or Nothing Options", binary options trading is a new alternative way of investing in options. It had gained tremendous popularity during the last few years. Its popularity is largely due to the fact that binary options are very simple to trade with. Unlike traditional options, traders of binary options only need to predict the direction of the option's underlying asset price in order to profit from their investment. Furthermore, the returns of binary options are predetermined allowing traders to quantify their investment risk.

Binary Options History

Binary options were a recent introduction in the financial markets. It made its debut into the mainstream financial world in when the Options Clearing Corporation proposed to the SEC to allow binary options to be traded in the mainstream markets. Hence, following a rule change, the American stock exchange and CBOE began to publicly offer binary options to the markets in 2008. Initially, binary options trading were just limited to contracts on the S&P 500 and CBOE Volatility Index. However as the market matured, more and more binary options contracts were offered to be traded covering a diverse range of underlying assets.

Why Trade in Binary Options?

Book smallBecause of the unique characteristics of binary options, they represent an excellent way to invest in the complex and confusing financial markets. As there are only two possible outcomes for binary options, in-the-money or out-of-the-money, traders don't have to worry about the unlimited risk factor that they faced trading with traditional options.

Returns are known beforehand and there is a wide choice of assets available for the trader's investment consideration. And because binary options contracts cover the four (4) main financial markets, trading is available 24/6. In the event of a trade being unsuccessful, some binary options brokers also offer a refund up to 15% of invested capital to traders.

With high payouts, easy access to the markets and the availability of trading regardless of the time of day, it is no wonder that the binary options market is attracting so many "greenhorns" to invest in the financial markets.

When to Trade Binary Options?

CalendarDespite claims to the contrary by same unscrupulous brokers, you should only start trading in binary options once you have grasped the basics of fundamental and technical analysis. You also have to ensure that you have sufficient prior planning before jumping into the water.

As binary options are quick expiring options, this usually leaves you very little time to contemplate on the best time to enter the market. Nevertheless, there are some strategies that you can follow to assist you in deciding when the best times to trade in a binary option are:

- Trade Based On Important Economic News
- Trade When The Major Markets Are Opened
- Trade According To The Trend
- How to Trade in Binary options?
- One, two, three, Trade!

With the technological advancement in the World Wide Web in recent years, it is now relatively simple for you to start trading in binary options.

The first thing that you need to do is to find a reliable binary options broker and open a trading account.

After opening a trading account, select an asset that is creating excitement in the market. (This should be based on the techniques that we will discuss later in this guide.)

Once you have decided on what asset to trade in, select the time-frame that you want to trade in.

Decide on the amount that you want to invest in.

Once you have gone through the above steps, just sit back and wait to see if your trade expires in-the-money or if you made a loss.

CHAPTER 1: ADVANCED

STRATEGIES OF BINARY

OPTIONS

MACD & Bollinger Bands Binary Trading Strategy

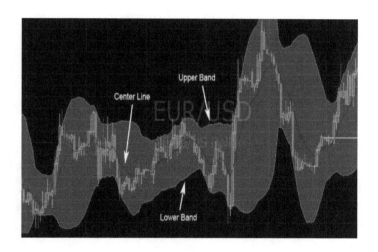

This strategy is an expansion of the MACD trading strategy. While the MACD is used for identifying the prevailing trend, this strategy adds the Bollinger bands as an additional indicator for a trade trigger in order to minimize the likelihood of a false signal. Although the MACD indicator is reasonably reliable, it is not without its shortcomings. One of its shortcomings is the fact that a wild price swing can result in prices varying significantly for the market trend. Another shortcoming of the MACD is because the indicator is a lagging indicator. And because of this lag, the MACD is susceptible to false signals as signals are generated only after prices have bottomed out or peaked.

The Bollinger Bands

A creation of by a technical analyst by the John Bollinger, Bollinger Bands comprises of an exponential moving average acting as a center line flanked by two price channels, an upper band, and a lower band. These bands will contract or expand as prices decrease or increase in volatility respectively.

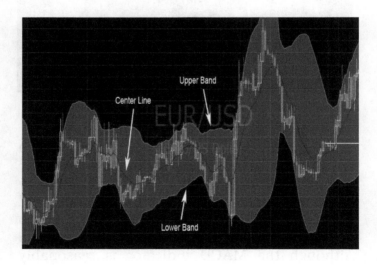

Analysts use the Bollinger Bands as a mean to help trace how the market is trading by filtering out the price action. Regardless of how prices are fluctuating, analysts are still able to monitor if the trading activities are still confined around the primary trend. Hence by using the Bollinger Bands, traders can hope to cancel out the effects of false signals as a result of wild price swings.

Advantages of the MACD & Bollinger Bands Strategy

There are several advantages of using this double indicators strategy to trade binaries. First of all, the MACD is a fairly dependable indicator for generating trading signals. It is reasonably accurate and simple to use. It allows traders to have an insight into what is happening in the market.

Secondly, the Bollinger Bands is a powerful tool especially for binary trading as it is an enveloping indicator. Regardless of which direction the market is heading towards to, traders can depend on it to trade the market. In addition, it cuts down the risk of false signals.

Lastly, this double indicators strategy is able to provide traders with precise market entry points making it easy to trade dynamic and volatile financial markets. Even though traders generally have difficulties is determining when to exit the market, this strategy is still able to provide them with some indication of where the exit points should be.

Disadvantages of the MACD & Bollinger Bands Strategy

Like all trading strategies, there are always some limitations to them. Likewise, the MACD & Bollinger Bands strategy is no exception. While this strategy is great for trading short term inaries like 60 seconds options, it becomes riskier as we stretch the timeframe of the trade longer.

The Bottom Line

Although the above-mentioned strategy helps to reduce the incidences of false signals, it doesn't entirely eliminate them from cropping up. Further analysis is required if traders wish the chances of acting on false signals.

On the whole, the MACD & Bollinger Bands strategy is quite effective especially when we are dealing with short-term binaries. But still, it is not without its own risks. But this is why we use double indicators as the readings from both indicators are used to confirm each other.

Interpreting the MACD Indicator for Binary Trading

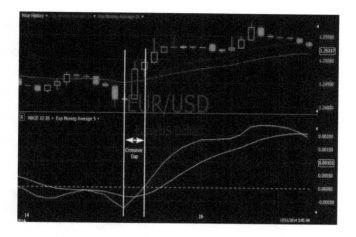

While the concept of binary options trading is a simple matter, to get ahead, a trader must be able to formulate an effective trading strategy on his own. In this article, we will take an in-depth look at how we can use the Moving Average Convergence Divergence (MACD) technical indicator to further our trading advantage when trading Call/Put binaries. Analysts generally use the MACD indicator to help them understand the magnitude of the momentum in the market.

The MACD uses the relationship between a shorter moving average of prices and a longer moving average of prices to discerning the momentum of a trend. It is derived by deducting 26 days exponential moving average (EMA) from 12 days EMA. To act a trigger for a trading signal, a 9 days EMA is then plotted over the MACD.

83

Interpreting the MACD Indicator for Binary Trading

The diagram below shows an example of what a MACD and the signal line will look like on a candlestick chart.

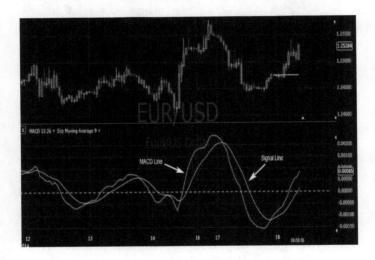

However, if the MACD is to be of any use, you need to be able to interpret it correctly and know what each signal is supposed to indicate.

Crossovers:

Crossovers between the MACD and the signal line can occur from above or below the signal line. If the crossover is from below the signal line, this is taken as indicative of a bullish signal. On the other hand, if the crossover is from above the signal line, this is taken as a bearish signal

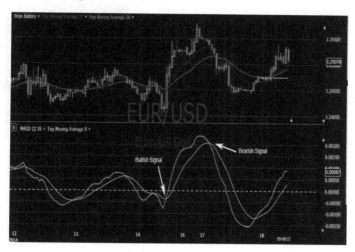

Entry Signal:

With reference to the figure below, since the crossover of the MACD and signal line occurs faster than the crossover of the two EMAs, there will be a slight gap between the two crossovers. You can use this crossover gap as an advance signal for entry into the market.

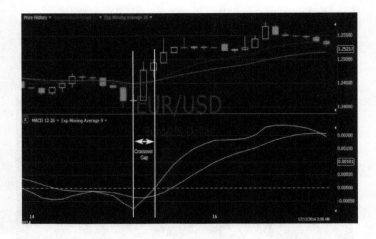

 As to whether you should purchase a Call option or a Put option, this will depend on whether the crossover is bullish of bearish. If the signal is bullish, buy Call options immediately after MACD and signal line crossover point. Conversely, if the crossover is bearish, buy Put options right after the crossover point.

While the MACD is an excellent indicator, you must be careful not to put too much emphasis on it. This is because a price shock could easily cause the prices to vary significantly from the prevailing trend. In such a case, it is always prudent to reconfirm your trading signal with another indicator before deciding to act.

CHAPTER 2: GAMMA SCALPING

STRATEGY FOR EXPERT BINARY

TRADERS

The binary options gamma scalping strategy is an advanced trading strategy for experienced binary options traders. Only traders who are extremely knowledgeable and well capitalized should ever consider using the gamma scalping strategy

Delta & Gamma

Gamma is a Greek term used to describe the rate of change of a financial option's delta as compared to the price of the option's underlying asset. Delta or "hedge ratio" in financial trading refers to the ratio of change of an underlying asset price as compared to the option's price. For an example of an option has a delta of 0.75, this mean for every $1 change in the price of an underlying asset, the price of the option will change by $0.75. So in other words, if an option has a gamma of 0.10, this mean the option will change by 0.10 delta as the price of the underlying asset changes.

Why Gamma Is Important

As an option moves more into the money, the bigger the option's delta will be and the more it moves out of the money, the smaller the option's delta will be. Since the price of an underlying asset is never constant in a dynamic market, this means an option's delta will also be constantly changing. Understanding the changes in the option's delta is crucial for a trader as it can affect the trader's bottom line. Hence, there is a need to keep track of an option's gamma.

The Gamma Scalping Strategy Explained

Basically, the gamma scalping strategy seeks to scalp gains through the adjustment of an option's delta by taking a long gamma position in times of shifting markets. In the financial markets if the volatility of an underlying asset is considered "too cheap", this is taken as meaning that the volatility of that underlying asset is higher than its market price. Under such a situation, it can be profitable for a trader to open an option position and move that position forward in the spot market since all such maneuvers have long gamma positions.

As mentioned earlier, when an underlying asset's price increases, its option's delta also increases. And if a trader has taken out a long option position and had hedged his position, he would also gain a long delta position from the consequent increase in the spot market. It is immaterial if the trader invested in a long put or call position since the option's delta will still increase with an increase in the underlying asset price.

In order to maintain a mean market position, a trader simply just have to buy puts if he wants to add to his position or sell calls to decrease his exposure and vice versa (depending on whether he is facing long deltas or short deltas).

Advantage and Disadvantage

The main advantage of the gamma scalping strategy is the fact that it cancels out the negative effect of time decay (theta) and collapses in the option's Vega. This is due to the fact that all gamma scalping strategies are affected to some extent by changes in liquidity and volatility.

However, the disadvantage of this strategy is the fact that a trader might need to wait for some time before making his anticipated move which will ultimately result in his position losing value due to theta. Nevertheless, trying to buy patience and to offset theta is the whole idea of the gamma scalping strategy.

CHAPTER 3: THE PIVOT BEAR TRADING STRATEGY

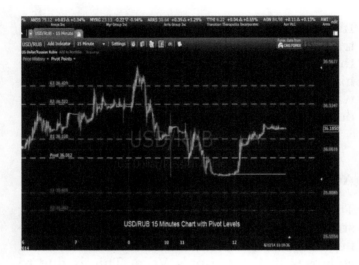

USD/RUB 15 Minutes Chart with Pivot Levels

Pivot Point Bear strategy is an excellent strategy not only for risk control when trading binary options but also can be used as an indicator or monitoring tool. Traders are advised to familiarize themselves with this strategy so they will provide them with a powerful tool in their arsenal of trading strategies

What Are Pivot Points?

By definition, pivot points are a type of technical indicator that is used by technical analysts to verify the primary market trend over a range of different time frames. It is essentially a point derived from the average of the previous day's high, low and closing price. For technical analysts, pivot points are mostly used for determining the resistance and support levels of a trend. In the analysis of pivot points, technical analysts calculate the first set of support and resistance level by using the asset's price range from the pivot point to either the asset's previous day high or low prices. As for the second set of support and resistance level, it is derived from utilizing the full range of the asset's previous day highs and lows prices.

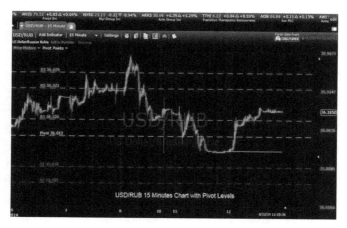

USD/RUB 15 Minutes Chart with Pivot Levels

Calculating Pivot Points

There are actually a few ways of calculating pivot points. One method is by the 5 points system as we have mentioned earlier above. With this system, in addition to 2 support and resistance levels, the asset's previous day closing price, its high and low prices (altogether 5 price points) are used to derive point.

Uses of Pivot Points

The pivot points derived can be utilized in 2 ways. Firstly, traders can use it to determine the primary trend in the market. If prices are breaching the pivot point price level in an upward manner, then the market is regarded as being bullish. If however, prices are breaching the pivot point level in a downward manner, then the market is seen as bearish. It should be noted that pivot points are essentially short-term indicators of the market trend. Its validity is only for a single day.

The second use of pivot point levels is an indicator as to when traders should enter or exit the market. For example, if prices are breaching a resistance level, this is the time that the trader should enter the market. On the other hand, if prices are breaching a support level, this mean the trader should get out of the market. A stop loss order can be set at this support level to be triggered if the level is breached.

Pivot Point Bear Trading Strategy

With the pivot point bear trading strategy, the goal is to capitalize on down trending market. To get an indication of the magnitude of prices moving downwards, the trader will use pivot point levels to plot the movement of price changes. With each passing day, the trader will be able to see how low prices are moving to. To confirm the bearish conditions of the market, traders can use the "inverted hammer" candlestick pattern as an indicator. Using the daily pivot point level as a threshold, if the opening price of the opening candlestick is below the threshold, then the trader can be fairly certain that the market is bearish with prices trending downwards for the day. The same principle can also be applied by traders wanting to trade a bullish market.

Regardless of whether one is a new or experienced trader, this trading strategy is simple and easy to apply. With enough practice, traders can easily obtain an accurate indication of the market trend for the trading day.

CHAPTER 4: USING CHANNEL

IDENTIFICATION IN BINARY

OPTIONS STRATEGY

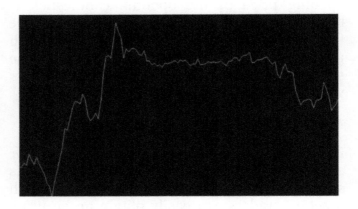

Traders dream about stumbling across an asset trading in a channel. It has all the advantages of trading with the trend, but also provides a bunch of signals which make trading really profitable. Channels are often hard to identify and carry a risk of breaking unexpectedly, which is why they often aren't discussed in many binary options strategies. But when they do appear, they can give the opportunity for substantial profit in a short time, which makes them worthwhile to discuss.

A channel is basically when the market get's confined between two trendlines. There are several reasons for why the market would behave like this, such as investor risk appetite, Fibonacci levels among others. But that's really advanced and is only useful to someone who spends all day tracking the market.

So how can you identify a channel? Well, this is what one looks like;-

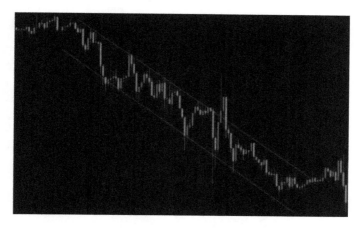

Notice how the market obligingly keeps between the two red lines, and each time it comes up to touch one, it backs off. Channels never last forever, so what you are looking for is to get in a few good trades while it lasts and always keep an eye out for what happened near the end when the channel ended. In this chart, you could have had up to 11 trades between puts and calls that would end up in the money.

As you can see, the principal advantage of a channel over trading a trend is that it gives you signals in both directions –whereas in trend trading you only get signals in one direction. This potentially doubles the number of trades you can make.

Catching a channel

Of course in that picture, it's pretty easy to identify the channel once it has already formed. The idea is to catch it in the beginning stages. To do that, we turn to our handy charting software and open a chart as a line graph. The reason is that the tops and bottoms of movements are easier to identify because a line graph only shows the close for each period. Here's what that chart above looked like as the channel was forming:

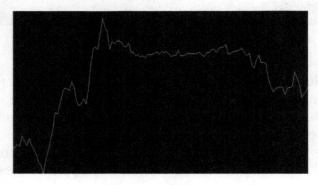

Near the end, it looks like there might be a downtrend forming. A trend, of course, is a great opportunity to trade on its own merits,

but if we want to see if the trend is sticking to the channel, we need to find three pivot points.

Pivot points are where the market changes direction, and they are conveniently indicated by the arrows. Any trading software worth its salt will have a channel tool that you can apply to the graph. You want to trace the channel tool over the two points that are on the same side. In this case, they are the two on top like this:

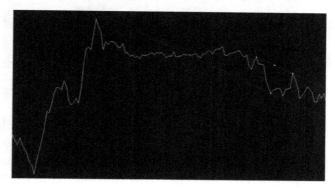

Note how the drawing points are placed on the points of the movements. If your software doesn't have a channel tool, you can draw a channel with two trend lines. Just remember that they have to be parallel, which can be a bit tricky to draw.

Then you want to switch your chart to Japanese candlesticks. You always have to be alert for the possibility that the market will break out of the channel, but in the meantime, you want to watch for when the market comes down to touch one of the sides of the channel. As long as the market stays in the channel that means it the market will move in the opposite direction and is a great opportunity to buy an option

If the market touches the top of the channel, you want to buy a put —expect the market to go down. If the market touches the bottom then you buy a call —expect the market to go up. Typically you'd set your chart to the same timeframe as the expiry of your options. For example, if the options expire every 15 minutes, then you want to chart in a 15 minute period.

This strategy works in conjunction with other trend strategies, giving you the second set of signals to either confirm the trend or show retracement opportunities.

CHAPTER 5: BINARY OPTIONS

FENCE TRADING STRATEGY

The Binary Options Fence Trading Strategy is designed to help traders reduce the risk of investment through the use of binary options. Basically, the strategy requires the purchase of two (2) options contracts on the same asset. This is because the trader needs to cover both sides of the market. Hence, he buys both "Above" and "Below" contracts to "fence" in the prices of the asset in between the strike prices of these two (2) contracts. With this strategy, the trader is able to reduce his investment risk and also profit from the market even without really having to choose which direction the market will go.

For example, an underlying asset is presently trading at $20. He predicts that the price of the asset will rise within the next 10 minutes and thus buys an "Above" contract for $1000 to expire in 30 minutes. Initially, the market moves in favor of the trader until unforeseen events cause prices to fall. If the trader does nothing, the value of his investment will start to decline and ultimately leaves the trader out of the money. But with the fencing strategy, the trader can reverse this undesirable situation and lock in his profit.

Suppose the trader purchase a "Below" contract for $1000 when the price was trading at $25 after dropping from the peak of $38 just a few minutes prior. Assuming the payout is 85%, and the expiration price of the asset is between $20 and $25, the trader will be able to collect on both contracts earning a total profit of $1700 ($850 + $850).

If the expiration price finishes ABOVE $25, then the "Above" contract is in the money while the "Below" contract is out of the money. However, if the expiration price finishes BELOW $25, then the "Above" contract is out the money while the "Below" contract is in of the money. In either case, the trader's losses are capped at $150 as the $850 profit from either contract will help reduce the loss of the $1000 investment capital.

The main danger of this strategy is when the expiration price is below $20 on the "Above" contract and higher than $25 for the "Below" contract since both contracts expire at different times (The "Below" contract is bought after the "Above" contract). In such a scenario, the trader will lose all his investment capital of $2000. In order to avoid such a scenario, the trader must ensure that his analysis is spot on. The fence trading strategy is a simple and good strategy to adopt when the conditions in the market are suitable for its implementation. Nevertheless, the strategy requires traders to have some decent background knowledge about the market in order for its successful implementation.

CHAPTER 6: FIBONACCI IN

BINARY OPTIONS TRADING

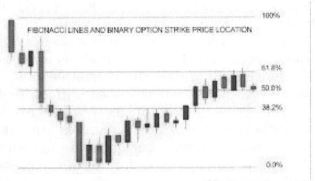

Fibonacci Lines and Strike Price Locations

The Fibonacci retracement tool is one of the lesser used technical indicators in market analysis, but still forms one of the best and most accurate strategies to accurately predict where prices are heading to.

Retracements are a regular part of trading. They happen all the time which means a trader needs to know how to use retracements to their advantage. This is where the Fibonacci retracement tool comes into play. The tool plots 5 horizontal lines on the charts which relate to 5 possible areas in which the price might retrace. The distances are expressed in terms of the percentage of the original move:

- 100%
- 61.8%
- 50%
- 38.2%
- 23.6%
- 0%

The Fibonacci sequence is essentially made up of a series of numbers where the 3rd number is the sum of the two numbers preceding it. An example is 0, 1, 1, 2, 3, 5, 8, 13, 21, and so on. It can be seen from the five levels above, the 23.6% and 38.2% levels are combined to provide the 61.8% standard. Once the charting tool is used with a pricing movement, these ratios stay true over any timeframe, providing high probability indicators into the areas where future levels of support and resistance might occur.

Once the price of the asset starts to indicate settling down, it is possible to see these as the levels where the prices will begin to show signs of stability.

Fibonacci retracements are at its best once the trader considers the trends in the market for an elongated time period. This might be difficult for the options with shorter times of expiry, but binary options trading now can involve month long options offered by many platforms.

Fibonacci ratios have proven to be a very useful tool for assessing the barrier points in binary options. However, as with any other indicator system, they are not flawless despite being more accurate than others. They can be an indicator of where traders are probably to act, but as with most forms of investment extra verification from other indicators would provide a more accurate guide to the interpretation of price action and increase the ability to correctly forecast future price directions. There are a number of varieties of free charting packages which will provide this information just a couple of clicks of the mouse away.

Overall, using Fibonacci in binary options is suitable ideally only when looking at the shorter term and is not best used for the longer term. They can be one of the most accurate and popular strategies to assist the trader in the shorter term where asset prices are moving towards.

CHAPTER 7: STRADDLE

STRATEGY

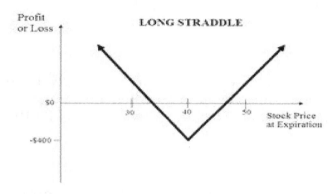

 The straddle is a trading strategy which involves the simultaneous use of put and call options with the same strike price and expiration date.

The straddle is a good trading strategy to adopt if you as an investor believe that the price of an underlying asset will fluctuate significantly but are unsure as to the direction of the fluctuation. For the straddle to be a profitable strategy, several conditions must be fulfilled first:

The price fluctuations must occur within a short term period.

The price swings must be significantly large.

There is an increase in implied volatility in the market.

If the price swings are not sufficiently large enough, then the profit earned might not be large enough to cover the premium paid for the options.

How to Profit From the Straddle Trading Strategy

For example, let us assume that you bought an EUR/USD 1.25 cent straddle for 4 cents expiring in a month time. If the EUR/USD rises to 1.35 cents, you would have gained 25 cents. Your total cost for the straddle is 4 cents for both the call and put (2 cents each). Because of the significantly large move in the price of the EUR/USD, you still have a net profit of 6 cents (10 cents – 4 cents = 6 cents).

Delta Hedging

Another way of profiting from the straddle is with "Delta Hedging". With Delta hedging, you reduce the risk linked to the price fluctuations of the underlying asset by equalizing your long and short market position. The investor risk exposure is zero with the delta hedge as he will not lose anything whether the market moves up or down. The only thing that he risks losing is the premium paid for the options.

Using the same example above, supposing the EUR/USD move from $1.25 to $1.30 and then back to $1.25. Let's suppose this fluctuation is repeated twice during the one month period which you own the straddle. When the EUR/USD price reached $1.30, it is possible to delta hedge at $1.30 with the anticipation that the market will continue to move. As the market move up, you become longer on the call and vice versa on the put. To remove this risk, you need to short the market and hence removing the delta. If the fluctuation occurs twice, you will be able to reap a profit from the price increase of $1.25 to $1.30 twice and $1.30 to $1.25 twice giving you a total profit of 20 cents on the delta hedge. This gain is more than sufficient to cover the losses that you incurred on the premiums.

Implied Volatility

An increase in the implied volatility of the market is another which you could gain from the straddle. The value of an option is determined by the implied volatility of the market. With an increase in the implied volatility of the market, the value of the option will naturally increase.

CHAPTER 8: DRAW DOWN

STRATEGY

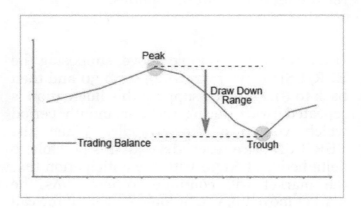

p Draw Down is for intermediate and advanced traders and is a key concept

A draw down happens when a trader's investment capital is reduced after a streak of losing trades. It is measured by the difference between the peak of one's invested capital (equity capital) to that of a trough in one's invested capital.

Implication of Draw Down for Traders

As binary options traders, we are always looking for that extra edge to get us ahead in our trading. To do so, we develop trading systems to achieve this aim. So if we managed to develop a system which 70% profitable, theoretically this would mean that for every 100 trades, we would come out ahead 70 times. However, in the real world, things are not as clear-cut. Who is to say that we won't lose 30 times in a row before we start winning? This leaves us with an important question to think about. "Would we still be in the game after the 30th time of losing trades?"

Draw Downs are an intrinsic part of financial trading. This is the reason why we have to carefully manage our investment funds in order to be able to pull ourselves through a losing streak. Furthermore, each time a drawdown happens, we need to make more in terms of percentage to recuperate what we lost initially.

In the above example used earlier above, we lost 50% of our initial trading balance. Why?

We initially started off with $100,000. After a 50% draw down, we are left with $50,000. This mean to make back what we lost, we need to make $50,000 which is now 100% of our remaining investment capital. If we had stuck to the idea of recuperating just 50% back, we would have only recuperated $25,000. Add this amount to our remaining capital of $50,000 gives us only a total of $75,000, a net loss of 25% actually.

The table below summarizes what percentage return is needed to recover funds lost after a draw down:

Percentage Loss

Percentage required after Draw Down

- 10%
- 11%
- 20%
- 25%
- 30%
- 43%
- 40%
- 67%
- 50%
- 100%
- 60%
- 150%
- 70%
- 233%
- 80%
- 400%
- 90%
- 900%

This is why it is important for traders to have good money management skills to limit their drawdowns and balance their risk-reward ratio to what is prudent and acceptable.

Causes of Draw Downs

One reason for draw downs is because of losing streaks which cause a trader suffers one loss after another. Another more significant reason for draw downs is because of a large winning market position reversing and breaking its trend. Successful trend trading strategy calls for a trader to continue trading until it breaks. Normally when a trend starts to break out, the trader will start adding to his market position until towards the end he becomes heavily invested. This is great if the trend continues but as we all know, all trends will eventually start to reverse. It is at this point of time that the trader will suffer considerable draw downs if he is not prepared for this eventuality.

Trading To Minimize The Impact Of Draw Downs

One strategy which traders can adopt to help them minimize the impact of draw downs is to adopt which is known as "Reverse Pyramiding". As opposed to "Standard Pyramiding" which calls for the trader to keep adding to a market position while it shows strength, reverse pyramiding calls for unwinding one's market position after a strong run. So if you are riding on a trend and becomes heavily invested in that trend, you should start to divest your market position once the market starts to pull back.

For example:

Supposing your portfolio had dropped by 5% since its peak, you start to scale back your portfolio by 25%. With reference to our example used above, if the peak of your portfolio was $100,000 and it had dropped to $95,000 (5% draw down), you should start to reduce your portfolio to around $71,250 (25% of $95,000). For every 5% drop in the value of your portfolio, you would continue to reduce your holdings by a quarter.

If you continue to reverse pyramiding in this manner, you will find that the maximum drawdown that you will experience is 20% as you liquidated your holdings by 25% each time a 5% draw down is experienced. With this strategy, as your holdings become smaller, it gets harder and harder for your portfolio to be significantly affected. in fact, it would be next to impossible to touch the maximum 20% draw down as you would have exited most of your market position. Reverse pyramiding is a very simple tool to use but it is also extremely effective in helping traders minimizing their drawdowns while maximizing their profit potential

CHAPTER 9: COLLAR STRATEGY

– PROTECTIVE OPTIONS

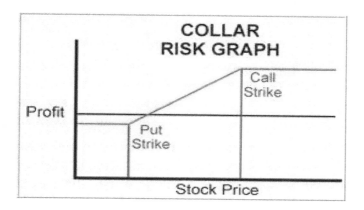

In the trading of financial instruments, you will always run the risk of losses whenever the market does not react or perform as anticipated. To help you minimize this risk, you can use a trading strategy commonly known as a "collar strategy". It involves reversing your risk by purchasing a call option and selling a put option or purchasing a put option and selling a call option.

As mentioned earlier, a collar trading strategy is used when you want to recuperate some of the transactional costs of a purchased option. This can be done by taking a market position in the opposite direction, i.e. selling an option. The attractive part of this strategy is that in certain situations, it is possible to completely offset price that you paid for the option resulting in what is known as a "costless collar". For example, let say you purchased a call option for a premium of $1.75. For this scenario to be a costless collar, you will need to sell a put option (for the same trading period) that has a price of $1.75 in order to totally offset the premium ($1.75) paid for the call option that you purchased earlier.

You normally use the collar trading strategy when you are unsure of the underlying price fluctuations. It is, in essence, a multi-legged protective trading strategy. What the collar does is to lock you into a protected price range. Downside protection comes into play when the strike price of the underlying asset falls below the strike price of the put option. However, you will forfeit any profit that is above the call option strike price.

As mentioned earlier, the collar trading strategy is a multi-legged trading strategy. Nevertheless, it can also be applied a single leg at a time. Earlier on, we also

mentioned that it was possible for a collar to be costless, a situation where the money received from selling calls equal the premium paid for the puts. However, collars can also be structured in such a way that you can receive a premium or pay out some premium. The reason for structuring a collar that pays out some premium is due to the fact that you get to minimize your risks further by being able to liquidate an option that is further out of the money.

To illustrate this concept better, let's look at an example below:

Let's us assume that ABC Corporation is trading at $79. You purchased an ABC $88 call option with a bid price of $1.75. Supposed you simultaneously sold an ABC $88 put option also for $1.75. In this case, your collar will be a costless collar ($1.75 Call option bid price – $1.75 Put option bid price).

If we expand the above example further, you will end up paying some premium out if you had sold an ABC $85 put as the bid price would naturally be lower than $1.75. Let's assume the bid price for the $85 put is $1.24, this would mean that you will be paying out a premium of $0.51 ($1.75 Call option bid price – $1.24 Put option bid price). The end result of this collar is to allow you further room to maneuver until $78 instead of $88 as in the first instance.

It is always beneficial for a trader to trade using the collar strategy. As an investor, you will get to reduce the risk that is intrinsic in a volatile market with the collar. At the same time, you also benefit from not having to fork out a substantial sum for the benefit of mitigating the adverse effects of a volatile market. Although the collar is an interesting trading strategy, you need to have a robust understanding of how the market works before you can start applying as part of your trading strategy.

CHAPTER 10: PROTECTIVE PUT

STRATEGY

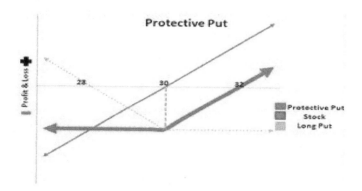

The Protective Put Strategy is for Advanced traders

Now let's learn how to use the protective put strategy. For those who are new to options, a "Put" option is a contract which gives the holder of the option the right to sell an underlying asset at a specific price within a specific time frame. It, however, does not impose any obligation on the holder of the option if he decided not to exercise the right.

Unlike a put buying strategy where the investor is selling short in the market, a protective put strategy is a strategy used by investors to minimize their risk profile

How the Strategy Works

As mentioned earlier, a put option allows an investor to sell an underlying asset at a predetermined strike price in exchange for the premium paid for the put option. For example, by purchasing an August 500 Gold put option for a premium of $1000, this entitles you to sell a gold futures contract at 500 per ounce on or before its expiration date in August.

With a protective put strategy, your risk is limited to the premium that you paid for the put option which in our example used is $1000. What differentiates a protective put strategy from a put buying strategy is the fact that the investor is buying the put option for the underlying asset which he already owns. The strategy is used to protect an investor's accumulated profit rather than his investment capital.

A Protective Put Strategy Example:

Let us assume that you own 100 shares of ABC stock bought at $50 per share. Ignoring commissions paid, your stock portfolio would require an investment of $5000 ($50 x 100 shares). Let's further assume that 3 months later the price of ABC stock has risen to $85 per share. This would translate into an unrealized profit of $3500 ($8500 − $5000).

Normally to lock in your profit, you would have to liquidate your portfolio. The main disadvantage of doing this is that it prevents you from reaping further gains should the stock prices increase further.

With a protective put strategy, you can overcome the dilemma of having to liquidate your stock portfolio. Your profits are locked in as you acquired the right to sell your stock at $85 with the put option you purchased. In return for this insurance, you pay a small premium for the put option. So your total risk is just limited to the premium paid for the put option.

The philosophy behind the protective put strategy differs from the covered call strategy in two main ways. First, the protective put strategy calls for you as the investor to purchase the put option for a premium. The covered call strategy calls for you to sell a call option to receive a premium. Second, the protective put strategy is more suited to markets which are high volatile. The covered call strategy is geared more towards the market with relatively low volatility. As mentioned earlier, the main goal of the protective put strategy is risk mitigation for an underlying asset or portfolio thus it is not surprising to sometimes find investors combining the use of this strategy with the covered call strategy.

Chapter 11: Covered Call

Strategy

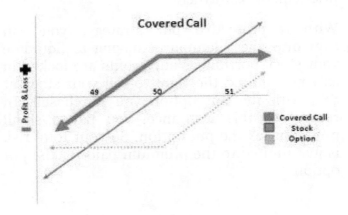

One of the ways which you can reduce your trading risk is to employ the use of the covered call strategy. The strategy is specifically used is a situation when you are holding a long market position in an asset. In order to reduce the risk in this situation, you can write (sell) a call option on that asset. The idea of this is to generate additional income (option's premium) from the asset traded by selling the option later. An incidental benefit of this strategy is that you also get to minimize the extent of your losses if the market suddenly tanked

Call Options Defined

In order to fully understand the concept of the Covered call strategy, it is important to have some basic knowledge about what options are. Options are essentially financial contracts that give the holder of the option the right to buy or sell a particular asset at a specific strike price on or before the date which the option will expire. It should be noted that the option does not oblige the holder to exercise these rights.

With a Call Option, the holder of the option gets to buy an asset at the stated strike price on or before its expiry. Let's say that you strongly believe that the

USD/JPY trading at 98.20 will rise higher in the short term. You can benefit from this rise by purchasing a near term USD/JPY Call Option that allows you to buy the USD/JPY at the current rate of 98.20. In the event the USD/JPY does rise higher to say 115.00, exercising the call option will allow you to profit from the exchange rate differential, in this case, 16.8 yen (115.00 -98.20). Supposing the anticipated rise in the USD/JPY did not occur, in this case, you can choose not to exercise the call option. Your loss will then be just limited to the premium that you paid for the near term USD/JPY Call option.

Naked Call Vs Covered Call

In the above example, we discussed how call options work. On the other side of the equation, there is also the seller of the option who assumes the unlimited risk. Thus when you as an investor become an option seller, you will actually be assuming an unlimited level of risk especially in "naked call" scenarios. A "naked call" is defined as a situation where an option seller sells an option without owning the underlying asset for the option.

In order to mitigate the risk level, the covered call strategy can be employed. In essence, a covered call strategy requires the option seller to own the underlying asset so the call option is backed or covered by actual ownership of the asset. Thus, in the event the market moves against you and the call option get exercised, you are hedged against unlimited losses.

At this stage, you might be wondering why to bother dealing with covered call options and not just deal in the underlying asset only. Well, the thing is with covered call options, even if the option that you sold get exercised forcing you to sell the underlying asset at the strike price, you will still get to earn the premium from the option sold.

For example, let's say you own several lots of USD/JPY. You decided to sell call options for the USD/JPY for a premium of 50 cents with a strike price of 110.00 while it is still trading at 98.00. So if the USD/JPY doesn't move beyond 110.00, you will have earned the premium of 50 cents from the options sold. However, if the USD/JPY moves beyond 110.00 (the strike price), then you will be forced to sell the USD/JPY at 110.00 to the holder of the call options. As you can see in this scenario, the risk is mitigated as you already owned USD/JPY and you also get to earn additional income (premium) from the options sold.

Although the covered call strategy can be quite a complex strategy, nevertheless it is a good strategy to employ when you want to:

Earn a premium from selling a call to assume the obligation of selling an underlying asset at a specified price.

Take profit only at a level which is above the current price level.

Forsake the upside profit potential in return for some downside protection.

CHAPTER 12: A GREAT BINARY OPTIONS STRATEGY- LONG BOX TRADING

To become a successful binary options trader, one doesn't need to be a rocket scientist. All it takes is some basic mathematical skills and a mind that is capable of making straightforward analysis. For the Long Box trading strategy, a trader will be concerned about buying simultaneous purchase and selling of a call and put options with identical strike prices and expiration times respectively. The strategy is normally adopted by traders when the options are underpriced in comparison to their expiration values. In other words, the trader can lock in profit immediately if the premiums paid for the call and put options is substantially lower than the combined expiration value of the options.

Although the long box strategy may sound complex initially, it is in essence no different from many other trading strategies which a trader may employ during the course of his trading. The basic essence of all trading activities calls for the buying and selling options until a trader's profit level reaches to a certain level of the expiration value. To sum it up, the long box trading strategy is about:

- Higher Strike Price – Lower Strike Price = Expiration Value of Box
- Expiration Value of Box – Net Premium Paid = Risk-free Profit
- The Benefits Of The Long Box Trading Strategy
- Ability to convert overpriced options to profits
- No fear in implementing this strategy as it is risk-free.
- Earn instant risk-free profit even though the gain might not be huge.

Disadvantages Of The Strategy

Must be vigilant with regards to the premiums and possible payout.

Need to perform a market analysis to look for overpriced options.

Traders cannot hope for a large gain.

As the possible gains from the long box strategy will not be large, traders need to bear in mind that all their gains could be wiped out if their broker charges a high spread. This obviously isn't so relevant with binaries as the trader is not usually charged a spread in any case.Hence, a trader cannot afford to let his guard anytime while he is using this strategy.

CHAPTER 13: MONEY MANAGEMENT – STOP LOSS AND PROFIT TAKING

Stop Loss and Profit Taking is for the intermediate and advanced traders

Before beginning to trade in the financial markets, you must have your money management strategy sorted out first. This involves allocating sufficient trading capital and deciding how much money that you are willing to lose. You also need to devise a proper trading strategy that allows for a realistic risk to reward ratio using stop loss techniques and take profit.

Ideally, the risk to reward ratio should be one where the profit level is at least three times that of the amount you risk. That mean to earn $3, the maximum that you should risk is only $1. Mathematical speaking, with a 3 to 1 ratio, you will need to have a trading strategy that will win more than 25% of the time.

For example:

Let say out of 8 trades, we win 2 times (2 x $3 = $6) and lose 6 trades (6 x $1 = $6). This mean our profits will be canceled by our losses.

So in order to have any gains, we need a trading strategy that will allow us to win more than a quarter of the time.

Never ignore this important trading philosophy about balancing your risk to reward ratio. If you do so, you will just end up losing money in the long run.

Stop Loss As Part Of The Risk Management Strategy

As part of your risk management strategy, you need to consider how much that you are willing to risk based on your allocated investment capital. This translates into how much market swing that you are willing to accept against your market position. Once you have decided on this, you will able to use an important tool for risk management, the stop loss order.

The stop loss order lets a trader stop out of a trade when prices reached a predetermined level. It can be based on a percentage move in market prices or potential dollar amount of money lost.

There are several ways of determining where to place the stop loss order. It can be based on historical movements of prices, technical analysis or just purely on a theoretical dollar amount of losses that you can bear.

With strategies based on historical movements of prices, traders have the advantage of backtesting a range of stop loss amounts to see which the best stop loss level is for them.

Technical analysis also provides a very reliable way of determining a stop loss level. Used in conjunction with trendlines, support and resistance lines provide a good graphical illustration on where a stop loss level could be placed.

From the chart illustrated below, the investor here has decided to place his stop loss at the recent low to protect his profit level.

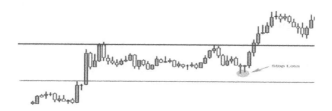

Beside from support and resistance levels, there are also other indicators like trend lines, moving averages which a trader can employ to help him decide where to place his stop loss.

Another important aspect of stop loss is that it can be dynamic. This mean an investor can set his stop loss in accordance with a percentage movement in the market. This type of stop loss is known as a trailing stop loss.

Profit Taking

Equally important for a trader is knowing when to exit a trade. This determination should be made beforehand just like the determination on how much to risk. Just like the way you determine your risk level, profit taking can be based on a theoretical dollar amount, as a percent of market movements or purely based on a level determined through technical analysis. Using the support and resistance lines is an excellent way of determining your profit level.

Regardless of the profit level, you should always make this determination in conjunction with the amount of money that you are willing to lose. Always avoid placing trades where your risk reward ratio is negative.

Chapter 14: Risk and Bet

Size Hedging and Stop Loss

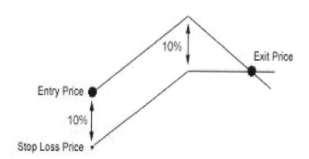

Manage Your Risk with Trailing Stop Loss

Trailing stop loss is used by investors to ensure that their risk to reward profile remains the same even after the market has moved higher. Compared to the fixed stop loss, the trailing stop offers one key advantage. It continues to protect an investor's trading capital even when the market drops. At the same time, because of is trailing feature, the investor is able to maximize his profit potential without having to sacrifice his risk protection level.

To understand the concept better, let us assume that the trailing stop loss is fixed at 5% of the amount invested or at a fixed spread of

20 cents. Regardless of whether it is a fixed percentage or at a fixed spread amount, the trailing stop is tied to the trading day's high by the predetermined ratio or amount. The crucial thing to note is that once the trailing stop level is set, it doesn't drop backward. For example, if the price happens to drop lower than the trailing stop value, it will trigger the stop loss.

One good thing about the trailing stop loss is that it helps to remove the emotional aspect of trading. The trailing stop loss value is usually set at the optimal level because the decision is usually arrived at after a calm and focused analysis of the information presented by the trading charts. There is no second guessing here. Nevertheless, there is the danger of setting the trailing stop too tightly that it is easily triggered by minor price drops causing investors to fret over "lost" profits.

Bet Size

Apart from mitigating your possible losses and maximizing your profit potentials with stop losses and take profit levels, you also need to consider your bet size in your trading strategy. The main idea of doing this is to preserve your trading capital so you can survive the rigors of the market to be able to trade the next day. Every experienced trader knows that returns commensurate with risk. The higher the risk level, the higher the returns. However, there is a thin line between trading for maximum profitability to trading with greed. As the famous Wall Street saying goes, "Bulls make money, bears make money, pigs get slaughtered".

The question is how much capital should be risked in a trade? If we risked too little, our return would hardly be significant to make any dent in our ending balance. If we risked a large amount, we run the risk of incurring a large loss which could possibly deplete our investment capital.

To help traders determine the appropriate amount to invest, they have relied upon several mathematical models to help them deal with the impasse between risk and return.

The Monte Carlo Simulation model uses historical back-testing to see what the optimal bet size is. The Kelly formula, on the other hand, assigns fixed ratios of capital to be invested in each trade based on their long-term capital growth. The Fixed Ratio method discussed by Ryan Jones in his book "The Trading Game" tries to balance geometric growth against risk. This method tries to mitigate the risk level by adjusting the trade size downward.

The fact is there is no foolproof money management model. Each of the mathematical models mentioned above suffers from limitations in one form or another. The models are not able to fully integrate the risk element into their calculations. For methods that placed a secondary importance on the relationship between risk and capital losses, they run the risk of making traders complacent about the degree of risks involved in trading.

At the end of the day, it doesn't really matter if the strategy used is systematic or discretionary one. What is more important for you as a trader is to create a trading strategy which allows you to manage your investment capital in a distinct manner. This is one of the keystone foundations in ensuring that your trading strategy is a successful one.

You have to remember that the end goal is to ensure that your investment capital remains relatively intact. You want to be able to place trades over a period of time and not have your trading career cut short due to massive draw downs. Finding the optimal bet size is not an easy task but your trading strategy must be flexible enough to allow you to determine your "Uncle Point", that is the point where you find out if your trading strategy really works or not.

Managing Your Portfolio

Referred to as an art as well as a science, portfolio management involves the delicate task of balancing the risk undertaken to maintain the portfolio to maximizing its return. This includes having a range of diversified investment to help reduce the risk involved. As an investor, you do not want to get into a situation where you hold several market positions which are highly correlated. Having highly correlated investments mean an adverse move in one position could affect all the correlated investments. In short, you are essentially just holding a large single position which has the potential of suffering a large draw down.

Portfolio Hedging

Portfolio hedging in the process in which investors use a variety of strategies to help them reduce their portfolio risk exposure to negative directional movements in the market.

How Portfolio Hedging Work?

To hedge your portfolio, you need to use financial derivatives like options and futures to help you curb your losses. For example, if you are concerned about the short-term price fluctuations that can affect your investment, you can purchase put options to offset your losses with the profits from the put options. There are a large variety of options and futures that investors can use to hedge against price swings in stocks, commodities, currency pairs and changes in the interest rate.

As mentioned earlier, the end goal of hedging your portfolio is to curb against potential losses. This insurance, however, comes with a price because by hedging you also limit a number of potential profits that you could earn. Thus, it falls down to you as an investor to weigh the cost of hedging against the benefit that you might get in return.

CHAPTER 15: SCALPING: BINARY

OPTIONS STRATEGIES

In Cowboy movies, the word scalping holds a sinister meaning but in the world of online financial trading, it is a trading technique used by traders to skim profits from the financial markets. The main idea behind this trading technique is for traders to open a market position and close it within minutes once they have picked up just a few pips in profit. If we were to draw an analogy to this form of trading then it would be filling a bucket up by drip feeding. Because of their success rate traders can make thousands albeit at a slow rate, while many brokers tend to dislike scalpers. Although scalping is normally done by Forex traders, the same trading technique can also be employed in binary options trading.

Scalping with binary options is actually quite similar to scalping in Forex trading. The only main difference is that with binary options, the positions are closed automatically due to the expiry of the contract. Whereas scalping in Forex trading requires that the trader closes the market position.

Time Frame for Scalping

To scalp with binary options, traders need to use options with a short expiry time. Hence, the best options to employ for scalping would 60-second options. Although more and more binary options brokers are offering 60-second options trades, it should be borne in mind that not all brokers offer this type of trade. So check first if your broker offers this type of trade. Nevertheless, when 60-second options are not available, 15 minutes and 30 minutes binary options can also beutilized. Another way to scalp is by using Option Builder trades since Option Builder allows traders to determine the expiry time. Banc de Binary and Trader XP both offer the Option Builder platform

Tools for Scalping

Once you have decided on the time frame that you want to trade in, the next step is to determine the tools that you need before deciding to open a market position. Normally, the tools employed by scalpers include candlestick charts, price action analysis and technical indicators. Chart patterns analysis is not suitable as the analysis might yield the wrong analysis due to the longer time frame required. Only charts with a minimum time frame of 1 minute and a maximum of 15 minutes should be used if you want to employ scalping trading techniques. The main reason for this is so any information obtained from your analysis of the charts stays relevant. You don't want to analyze a 6-hour chart for a trade that is going to play out in just 60 seconds.

It all sounds pretty easy but remember that scalping is highly speculative. Practice often and be sure that you know what you are doing before you decide to start scalping! It's a fact that inexperienced traders end up with more losses than wins.

CHAPTER 16: THE FOREX MULTIPLE TIME FRAMES STRATEGY WITH BINARY OPTIONS

For this trading strategy, you will need a decent charting software and some patience.

Although trading with multiple time frames is not a new concept among traders in the forex circle, it is relatively unheard-of among binary options traders. Because binary options are normally traded with a relatively short time period, many traders choose to disregard multiple time frames trading. They think this trading system is not suitable for short-term instruments like binary options. However, losing sight of the bigger picture can often result in missing clear signals for probable market entry points.

Multiple Time Frames Trading System Explained

The multiple time frames trading system requires the monitoring of an asset's price movements across different time frames. Although there is no hard and fast rule regarding the number of the time frame required in this trading system, there are still guidelines that should be followed. Usually, three different time frames should suffice for a broad overview of the market. Using less than three-time frames will result in insufficient data for an inconclusive analysis while excessive time frames will only result in redundant analysis. When selecting the time frames to use, it is important to bear in mind "The Rule Of Four".

Medium Term Time Frame

The first stage of choosing your time frame is to select a medium term time frame which is representative of how long you hold your trade. So if you normally hold your trades for 6 hours (360 minutes), then that should be the time frame you use for your medium-term time frame.

Short Term and Long Term Time Frames

Bearing in mind the "Rule of four", your short term time frame should be 90 minutes (360 mins/ 4) while your long term time frame should be 24 hours (360 mins x 4). By following this basic guideline, we can see how we bring relevancy in our selection of time frames. Clearly, if you are holding a trade for around 6 hours at a time, there is no point having a 15 minute short term time frame chart. Otherwise, you will end up with 24 segments of 15 minutes chart to constantly review. The same reasoning goes for long term time frame selection.

Putting Theory To Work

In a multiple time frame trading situation, it is always best to do your analysis on a top-down basis. Hence, you will start your analysis on the long term time frame first and then work your way down to the medium term time frame and short term time frame respectively.

Long Time Term Frame

By looking at the long-term time frame, you can see the direction where the general trend is heading toward to. At this point, it is still too early to execute a trade. What should be noted is that when you do make your trade after all the analysis, it should be in the same direction as the general trend.

Medium Term Time Frame

As you focus more closely on the medium timeframe, spikes within the general trend will start to become more visible. The medium time frame is the most flexible frequencies among all the three-time frames as it is possible to get a sense of the short term and long term frames with it. Actually, it is also the time frame which most traders relied upon when planning their trades.

Short Term Time Frame

Your trades should only be concluded on this time frame. As you narrow down your focus to shorter time frames, you will notice that smaller price movements which are not so obvious before will become clearer. This will enable you to pick a vantage point to enter the market in the same direction of the general trend defined by the longer time frames.

When you combine all the analysis from the three-time frames, you will definitely improve the odds for a successful trade. A top down approach helps a trader to trade smartly in sync with the market trend. Poor trades due to temporary market fluctuations can be avoided entirely when trades are planned ahead in a progressive manner.

CHAPTER 17: IDENTIFYING

TREND REVERSALS

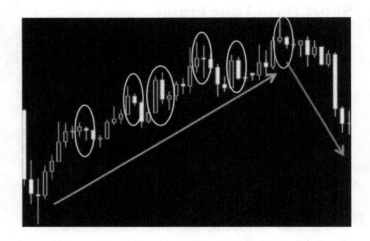

The trend is your friend is an oft-repeated maxim of trading, and a lot of binary options trading strategies hinge around identifying a trend and trading with it. Of course, every market is volatile, and every trend comes to an end. So, what do you do when the trend ends?

Knowing when to get into the market is an essential skill, but getting out at the right time is just as important. With binary options, it's a little easier to know when to get out, because they expire at a fixed time. But, if you are following a trend, how do you know if it's going to last until the option expires, and how do you know whether it's a good idea to get into another option right after, taking advantage of the continuing trend?

Let's take the following chart:

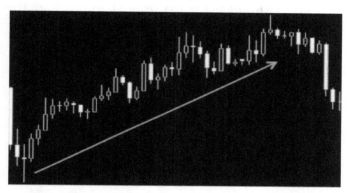

It shows a clearly defined rising trend. However, it didn't just go up and up but came across different pauses lung the way when it went down for a brief bit. These are corrections, and they happen in every market. The trouble is identifying when a change in direction is just a correction, or it's an outright reversal as we see at the end of the chart. This is even more important in binary options, because if you've identified the upwards trend, you don't want to get caught in one of those corrections.

Of course, there is no way of predicting the future, but there is a host of tools that investors can use to identify patterns that give an indication of when a reversal is imminent. A lot of them use sophisticated indicators like

Bollinger bands, Commodity Channel and Relative Strength indices, and the more exotic Ichimoku clouds.

But you can get a leg up by just looking at the graph.

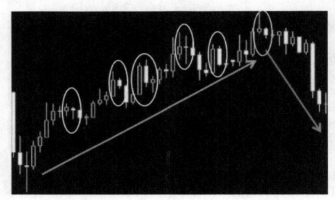

The movements on the graph can give you an idea of how strong a movement is, and often an indication of when a trend is starting to get exhausted. One of the more common indicators that an asset is in the process of reversing is that its downward movements become stronger than its upward movements.

This is a pattern called "engulfing"; either a "bullish engulfing" meaning the equity is about to start to go up, or a "bearish engulfing" meaning it will go down. They are the easiest to identify with candle or bar graphs, although you can spot them in a line graph with a very keen eye. Let's go back to the graph: Notice at each time the asset started a correction, the downward candle (bear candle) was shorter than the upward candle that preceded it (in other words, it went down less than it went up in identical time periods).

But later, when the trend reverses, the downward candle is longer than the preceding one, indicating that the downward movement is stronger. It's important to remember that this doesn't happen every time, but it can give you an edge in predicting when the market will turn around. This will allow you to prevent getting in on the wrong side of the trend, or be able to catch on to the new trend quickly.

CONCLUSION

Which Type of Binary Options Trader Are You?

Hey, Binary Options Traders, ask yourself this:

Binary options traders uncle samKnowing the kind of trader that you also help in the developing of your trading plan. So ask yourself which one of the following best suits your trading type:

A Day trader

Day traders only trade within the trading day with no overnight positions. Selections of trades are normally done at the start of the trading day. Most binary options traders fall under this category.

A Position Trader

Position Traders are longer term traders with trades spanning over weeks or months. Fundamental analysis plays a more important part here. If you are more comfortable in being a position trader, then binary options trading is not for you as it is fast moving with the trading period spanning several days at the most.

A Scalper

In contrast to position traders, scalpers' trades only last seconds or minutes. The main objective is to make as many trades as possible within the trading day. Here, volume rules over pips. This is the ideal category for binary options traders, especially those that trade using 60-second platforms.

A Swing Trader

Swing traders trades are normally over several days. Their trades are done with prior planning and then left to their own throughout the trading day. These traders normally do not have time to constant monitor their charts which why they adopt such a trading style.

Irrespective of your trading style, it is important that the style suits your lifestyle. Are you trying to make a second income? Perhaps trade over the weekends or is this your career?

Developing Your Own Trading Plan

Share this:Share via TwitterShare via LinkedInShare via FacebookShare via Google

Because of our individuality, we all have different attitudes, different experiences and different levels of tolerance to risk. By developing your own trading plan, you are cultivating one of the two main qualities that are needed from trading discipline. The other factor needed is being able to stick to your trading plan. With a rock solid discipline as your foundation, your goal as a successful trader is only a matter of time.

So What Is A Trading Plan?

A trading plan is a systematic way of executing your trade based on your market outlook and analysis after factoring in your personal psychology and appetite for risk. Always bear in mind that regardless of how well drafted your trading plan is, it is useless if you are unable to stick to it. It is only those who kept an iron clad disciplined approach towards trading survive the ups and downs of the market and still come out ahead. With a trading plan:

1. Trading is less chaotic as there is a roadmap to follow.
2. You have little stress as you are more in control of the situation.
3. You can monitor and track your performance and correct any shortcomings that you might have.
4. You will reduce the number of bad trades that you will make.
5. You can prevent any bad psychological bad habits from developing.

6. Trading outside the comfort zone is easy as you know what you are doing.
7. Any trading mistakes can be corrected quickly but things spiral out of control. Trading plans are developed to cater for various scenarios, best case, worse case and expected results.
8. A trading plan is dynamic. There is always room for improvements and adaptations. Nothing is set in stone. If the market situation requires you to adapt, then adjust your trading plan accordingly.

Keeping a Trading Journal

Keeping a Trading Journal is Crucial!

Although a tedious task, keeping a trading journal is crucial if you are aiming to be an effective trader. You need to be able to measure and keep track of your performance before you are able to improve and correct past mistakes. This is why having a proper journal is important.

Unless you have a photographic memory, it is impossible to remember all your trading details like reasons why you made a particular trade, why you selected a certain entry point or why you exited the market at a certain point. Even though you can refer to your trading or transaction logs provided by your broker, those data does not tell you the "reasons" for the trade. In other words, you cannot reflect back on your trading psychology.

For example:

Your trading plan calls for you to purchase the USD/JPY call options. However, your gut feeling tells you that this trade will not work and you are taking the trade because you are just sticking to your trading plan.

Later, halfway through the trade, you find that the market is starting to move against you and this sets you off thinking that why didn't you listen to your gut instinct in the first place. Prompted by the "demons" in your mind, you decided to close the trade early to minimize your losses.

Shortly after closing your trade, you find that the market has turned and is moving as expected according to your trading plan. The end result is that you could have turned a profit instead of suffering a loss. Without recording down the reason for the unplanned exit, you will never know that your emotion got the better of you here. With a written record in your trading journal, you will always be reminded that you must not let your emotion rule your trade.

Back Testing Your Binary Options Trading Strategies

Share this:Share via TwitterShare via LinkedInShare via FacebookShare via Google

Backtesting is where traders test their trading strategies using historical price data.

Instead of trading with new unproven trading strategies for the period ahead, a trader can use the relevant price data to simulate conditions to test the effectiveness of the newly developed strategy. The logic is if a trading strategy works well with historical data then it should also perform well in the future.

Backtesting is a critical part of trading system development as it is possible to structure rules on how the strategy should work using historical data. For example, you could base your strategy on an assumption that a specific asset tends to deviate away from its 20-period moving average by a few points away before sliding back to the moving average. With proper back testing, valuable information can be gained such as:

- Profit/Loss Levels
- Projected Returns
- Trading Success Ratio

The ultimate benefit that you will gain is confidence in the fact that your trading strategy is working properly before applying it in the real world. Before back testing, it is important to get the correct mix of price actions and technical indicators so the test will yield results of significance. Another point to remember about backtesting is to test your strategy over a long term period rather than just over small short time periods. This is to avoid a phenomenon known as "over optimization" where the strategy only works for the short-term periods but not over a broader range of time periods.

I wish you the best in your trading.

Jordon Sykes

Forex:

POWERFUL ADVANCED GUIDE TO DOMINATE FOREX

Jordon Sykes

Jordon Sykes

Introduction

I want to thank you and congratulate you for buying the book, *"Powerful Advanced guide to dominate Forex"*.

This book contains proven steps and strategies to excel at Forex trading with the use of advanced Forex concepts and advanced Forex strategies.

The $5.3 Trillion Forex market is figuratively a gold mine for anyone who is astute enough to identify and grab opportunities early in the game. In order to make consistent profits and avoid huge losses, you need two things in your arsenal —good understanding of advanced trading concepts, as well as a thorough knowledge about advanced trading strategies. If you are looking for a book that gives you both, look no further!

This book contains complex Forex strategies and concepts explained in a simple, easy to follow manner. Every strategy is detailed out and explained with the aid of examples and charts. This book will help you

- Identify which type of trading is best suited for you: Are you a Scalper, Intraday trader, or a Swing trader?
- Identify which are the important indicators and chart patterns.
- Pick out strategies best suited for the current market direction and your trading style.
- Avoid common pitfalls and mistakes

In addition, this book will also provide

- A one-stop reference for all basic concepts of Forex – you can simply read this book to refresh your Forex knowledge.
- Understanding of Fundamental and Technical Analysis.
- Expert Tips for becoming a successful Forex Trader.

Armed with the knowledge from this book, your trading is guaranteed to see a marked difference; as you will instinctively pick out trades that would maximize your profits. If you wish to change your Forex Trading for better by improving your trading strategies, we have got it covered!

Thanks again for buying this book, I hope you enjoy it!

Chapter 1: Brief Introduction to Forex Trading

Forex – It's all about the Money, honey!

Forex market, the abbreviation for Foreign Exchange Market, is where all the currencies of the world trade. Prevalently called as FX, it is the largest as well as most liquid investment market in the world.

Here are a few quick facts about Forex market

- Forex is traded over the counter and has no central exchange
- The average daily trading volume for FX is more than $5.3 Trillion
- Forex allows the buying and selling of currencies 24 hours a day, five days a week.
- Technically, there is no bear market in Forex, as you can make or lose money when the market trends up or down.

Before we get into the advanced concepts of Forex, let us do a quick recap of some of the important terminologies of Forex like Exchange Rate, Currency Pairs, Pips, Lots, and Leverage.

What is an Exchange Rate?

Assume that you are on a trip to Paris. Before you go shopping, you would be converting your dollars into Euros as soon as you reach France. The money you receive in Euros on handing over your Dollars is based on something called as the Exchange Rate.

This Exchange Rate keeps fluctuating on a daily basis, depending on the overall demand and supply. For instance, $1 USD could give you 0.89 Euros on Monday, while the same $1 USD could give you 0.90 Euros on Tuesday.

(Fig) Understanding Exchange Rates

If you check the above chart, it shows the Exchange Rate of USD relative to Euro over a period of five months. As you can see, the Exchange Rate keeps fluctuating.

What are Currency Pairs?

Remember the trip to Paris, wherein you exchanged Dollars for Euros? You were basically comparing the value of US Dollars to Euros. The USD/EUR is an example of a Currency Pair. Forex is generally quoted in pairs.

For example, USD/EUR at 0.89 shows how much one U.S Dollar (USD) is worth in Euros (EUR).

When quoting a currency pair, the first currency is called as the **base currency** or the **Commodity**. The second currency is called as **Counter Currency** or the **Money**.

(Fig) Currency Pairs

The most traded currency pairs are called as **Majors**. They usually demonstrate a high market liquidity as well as have the tightest spreads. All Major currency pairs have USD on one side.

The currency pairs that do not contain USD in either base currency or counter currency is called as **Crosses** or Cross Currency Pairs. The Crosses that contain EUR on one side are called as **Euro Crosses**.

Important Majors: EUR/USD, GBP/USD, USD/CHF, USD/JPY, USD/CAD, AUD/USD, and NZD/USD

What are Pips?

Price Interest Point, popularly known as **Pip** is used by Forex traders to quote the value of a currency pair. It is also known as a **tick**. A pip is the smallest change in the value of the exchange rate of a currency pair.

For example, if EUR/USD moves from 1.1286 to 1.1287, that movement is called as one pip. Currency pairs are usually quoted to four decimal places. The only exception is yen based currency pairs which are quoted with just two decimal places.

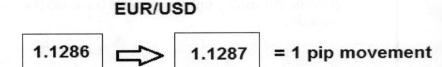

EUR/USD

(Fig) Pip Movement

Some brokers offer an extra decimal place when quoting the currency pair rates called pippettes. One pippette is equal to 1/10th of a pip.

What is a Lot?

A lot is basically the size of the trade that you make. One of the smallest lots is called as a micro lot and consists of 1000 units (1k units) of currency.

There are also mini lots which consist of 10,000 units, nano lots which consist of 100 units, and standard lots which consist of 100,000 units. Any trade can be made in **multiples** of these lot sizes.

Importance of Leverage

For small scale investors, trading such large amounts of money would be near impossible without a concept called as leverage. So, what exactly is leverage, and how does it help you trade?

Leverage is basically borrowed money. A leverage of 50:1 means that you can trade for $1000 in the Forex market by giving approximately $20 as the security deposit. The security deposit you provide (e.g., the $20) for holding the open positions is called as the *margin* requirement.

Now, this margin is not necessarily a fee or a transaction cost. It is basically a 'good faith deposit' set aside from your account's equity for maintaining your open positions. The amount of leverage varies from one broker to another.

But be warned that the leverage is like a double-edged sword. It can be used for taking advantage of even the smallest currency movements. At the same time, any losses encountered in trades would also be significantly higher.

Now that you have had a quick recap about important Forex terminologies, let us move on to other aspects of Forex like timings of trading sessions, global factors that impact Forex, and why Forex is getting increasingly popular.

Trading Sessions and best time to trade

Forex market opens at 5 pm EST on Sunday and closes at 5 pm EST on Friday. The chart below shows the timings of the various trading sessions for Forex.

Trading Session	Name of City	Open (EST)	Close (EST)
Europe	London	3:00 AM	12:00 noon
	Frankfurt	2:00 AM	11:00 AM
America	New York	8:00 AM	5:00 PM
	Chicago	9:00 AM	6:00 PM
Asia	Tokyo	7:00 PM	4:00 AM
	Hong Kong	8:00 PM	5:00 AM
Pacific	Sydney	5:00 PM	2:00 AM
	Wellington	5:00 PM	1:00 AM

(Fig) Trading sessions and their timings

The time when Forex market is most active is from the *opening of London session* until the *closing of New York session*.

The **peak** time for trading is the time when the two sessions (London and New York) overlap – which is from **8 am to 12 noon EST**. This is the ideal time for trading and maximizing profits.

Why should you trade Forex?

Forex has been gaining popularity, especially in the past decade when the internet became all powerful and made the Forex market accessible to even small investors. Here are a few reasons why you should trade in Forex.

- ***24 hours Availability:*** Forex market is available 24 hours a day. Hence, you can trade according to whichever business hours suits you the most.
- ***Can go long or short:*** Due to the high liquidity, you can either short or go long on a currency pair at any point in time. In other words, there is no bear market – you can make money (or lose it!) at any point in time.
- ***Availability of Leverage:*** Even when the movement of a currency pair is just under five pips, you can still make substantial profits due to the availability of leverage. Of course, the risk of losses is also quite high in such scenarios.
- ***Very low cost of trading:*** The broker commissions are lower and have a tight spread as well.

- ***International Exposure:*** The worldwide market is laid open for trading in Forex. So, if you are interested in investing or short selling the currency of a specific country, Forex is the best way to do so. The best part is that all this can be done while avoiding all the complicated foreign security laws and language barriers.

Types of Forex Traders

Forex traders can be broadly classified into three categories. They are – Scalpers, Intraday traders, and Swing traders.

So which type of Forex trader do you want to be? Which would be the most beneficial and profitable category of Forex trading for you? There is no clear-cut answer to the question, as it depends on your risk taking ability, time to execute trades and a host of other factors.

Let us now look at the three types of Forex traders and discuss then in detail so that you can have a better understanding of them.

1. Scalpers

Scalpers are basically traders who move in and out of a trade fairly quickly. Their holding time for a particular trade varies from a few a seconds to a few minutes. They take advantage of the volatility associated with the forex market and enter and exit a trade in a matter of minutes. They then repeat this process multiple times over the course of the day.

Scalpers take small profits per trade. But since they do it several times over the course the day, the final profit is by no means small.

Following are a list of qualities a scalper must possess in order to be a successful trader.

- He should have quick decision-making skills as he would need to enter and exit trades at the snap of a finger.
- He should be emotionally strong and should have the ability to trade like a machine without succumbing to emotions.
- He should have the mentality to accept and book losses quickly if the trade goes against him.

Below is the strategy that the scalpers use to book quick profits. Most scalpers use the combination of 5-minute and 1-minute time frame on the charts to look for trades.

First, check the current trend of the currency on the 5-minute chart. It can be either bullish, bearish, or neutral.

Bullish Trend

There are a few methods to check if the trend is bullish using the 5-minute charts.

1. If the candles are making higher highs and higher lows on the 5-minute chart, then the trend is bullish.
2. Another method is to check if the current price is above the 5 EMA (Exponential Moving Average) on the 5-minute chart. If it is above the 5 EMA, then it is bullish.

Once it is determined that the very short-term trend is bullish based on the 5-minute chart, look for entries based on the 1-minute chart. Here is how to do that.

Look for a reversal candle (e.g. hammer, doji, morning star etc.) that are formed on the 1-minute chart after a correction. Once such a reversal candle is formed, make an entry above the closing price of the reversal candle.

The stop loss should be a few pips below the low of the reversal candle.

So now comes the most important part, i.e. on how to make a quick exit. Various strategies can be used to do that but here is a simple strategy to do that – exit the trade once the 1-minute candle closes below the 15 EMA.

Bearish Trend

Following are the methods to check if the trend is bearish using the 5-minute charts

- If the candles are making lower highs and lower lows on the 5-minute chart, then the trend is bearish.
- Another method is to check if the current price is below the 5 EMA on the 5-minute chart. If it is below the 5 EMA then it is bearish.

Once it is determined that the very short-term trend is bearish based on the 5-minute chart, look for entries based on the 1-minute chart. Here is how to do that.

Look for a bearish reversal candle (e.g. hanging man, doji, evening star etc.) that are formed on the 1-minute chart after a pullback. Once the reversal candle is formed, make an entry below the closing price of the reversal candle.

The stop loss should be a few pips above the high of the reversal candle.

Exit when the 1- minute candle closes above the 15 EMA.

Neutral Trend

If the trend is neutral or in a range on the 5-minute time frame, then it's best to avoid doing scalping.

2. Intraday Traders

Unlike scalpers, Intraday Traders tend to hold the trades for a slightly longer timeframe – ranging from a few minutes to a few hours. Since the trader allows the trades to run for a slightly longer time in Intraday Trading, there would be fewer trades per day. But there would be more profits or losses per trade.

The ideal time frame to be used in intraday trading would be a combination of 3-minutes and 15-minutes. But this is not a hard and fast rule and many traders even use a combination of 5 minute and 30- minute timeframe.

The basic concept of Intraday Trading is the same as the one described in scalping. First, check the trend (bullish or bearish) on the higher time frame (15-minutes). Then, once the trend is determined, make an entry in the same direction as the trend using the lower time frame (3-minutes).

There are various strategies that can be used for intraday forex trading. A few of the advanced strategies of Forex trading will be discussed in detail with the aid of examples and charts later in this book.

Also, unlike scalping, Intraday trading can be done even when the trend is neutral or in a range. Some of the strategies ideal for ranging or the neutral market will also be discussed later on in this book.

3. Swing traders

Swing traders are the traders who are prepared to hold the forex trades for a longer time period when compared to the scalpers and the intraday traders. They typically hold the trades for a few hours to a few days. This depends on when the trend ends or when their exit condition is met.

In Swing trading, the profit potential is much higher as the trades are allowed to run for a longer period. But it should also be noted that the losses can be higher as well, as a wider stop loss needs to be set in order to prevent it being hit due to market volatility.

Another risk that the swing traders face is the losses during a gap up- gap down opening. Since the currency market is open almost 24 hours, there is that risk that the losses can pile up even after the currency session for your country is closed for the day.

There are various strategies that can be used for swing trading. A few of them will be discussed later in this book. The trading strategies for swing trading is also the same as intraday trading.

Chapter 2: Advanced Concepts of Forex

Now that you have had a refresher course on the basics of Forex, it is time to take it up a notch. In this chapter, you will be provided with the foundations of some of the important advanced concepts of Forex.

1. Average Directional Index

One of the important indicators used for determining if the currency price is trending or in a range is called as Average Directional Movement Index (ADX). It is basically used for quantifying the strength of the trend, and not the direction of the trend.

Average Directional Index is formed by the combination of three lines. They are - Plus Directional Indicator (+DI), Minus Directional Indicator (-DI), and ADX line.

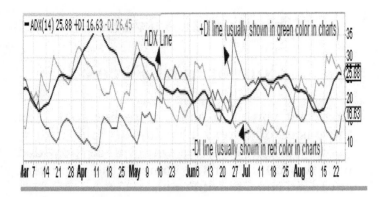

(Fig)   Components   of   Average
Directional index

The calculation of ADX is a complex one. But
most of the trading platforms have the ADX
indicator available by default.

How to use ADX to determine strength of trend

You can identify if the market is trending or
ranging depending on the value of ADX. Low
values   of   ADX   usually   depicts   an
accumulation or *distribution* phase. The
table below indicates how strong the trend is
depending on the value of ADX.

ADX value	Strength of Trend
<25	Weak
25-50	Strong
50-75	Very Strong
>75	Extremely Strong

(Fig) Strength of Trend based on ADX value

How to use ADX to identify Buy and Sell Signals:

According to the creator Welles Wilder, ADX can be used for identifying both buy signals as well as sell signals.

Buy Signal: Whenever (+DI) is greater than (-DI), and both ADX and (+DI) are above (-DI) and ADX is rising, it indicates a buy signal.

The exit point for this buy is when (+DI) cross below (-DI).

Sell Signal: Whenever (-DI) is greater than (+DI), and both ADX and (-DI) are above (+DI) and ADX is rising, it indicates a sell signal.

The exit point for this sell signal is when (-DI) cross below (+DI).

Let us now understand how to use Average Directional Index for buying and exiting a trade using an example.

In the below chart, the ADX line is the dark black line. The (+DI) as well as (-DI) line are annotated in the below figure for easy comprehension. Note that in the case of charting software, the (-DI) line would be red in color while the (+DI) line would be of green color.

In the following chart, when the (+DI) line crosses above the (-DI) line; a buy signal is triggered. This crossover point of (-DI) and (+DI) is noted in the chart. At the same point in time, the price starts to increase.

After two weeks, the (+DI) line starts to cross below the (-DI) line. This crossover point of (-DI) and (+DI) is also marked in the chart. This is the exit signal. In other words, this is the point wherein the buyer should take profits and exit from the trade. As soon as the crossover happens, you can see that the price starts to decrease.

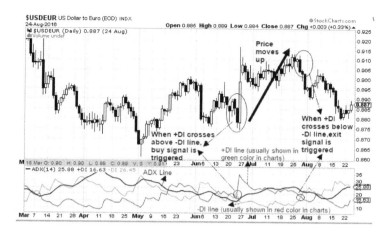

(Fig) Buy signal and exit signal using ADX indicator

2. Chart patterns

Since the price movements in a currency are affected by the crowd behavior, certain chart patterns tend to repeat itself. Hence, it is vital to have a good knowledge about these important chart patterns in order to enhance your trading success.

In the next section, you will be familiarized with some of the commonly occurring chart patterns. For ease of comprehension, these chart patterns are divided into Bullish Patterns, Bearish Patterns, and Continuation chart patterns.

2.1.. Bullish Chart Patterns

After the price of the currency declines for some time, certain external factors could result in reversal of the price. This is reflected by the formation of bullish chart patterns.

Some of the important bullish chart patterns are Inverted Head and Shoulders, Rounding Bottoms, Double Bottom, and Triple Bottom formation.

2.1.1. Inverted Head and shoulders pattern

The Inverted Head and Shoulders formation happens at the end of a long decline in the price of the currency. The formation of this pattern predicts a trend reversal from the existing downtrend.

How to identify Inverted Head and Shoulders pattern?

When the price action of the currency happens in the following manner it is set to form an Inverted Head and Shoulders pattern.

The currency would be in a downtrend initially. In the first step, the price falls down and rises again, creating a trough. This becomes the first shoulder, also called as the left shoulder.

After the formation of left shoulder, the price falls down and rises again, creating a deeper trough. This becomes the head.

In the third and final step, the price falls down and rises again but not as deep as the second trough. This becomes the second shoulder, also called as the right shoulder. Thus the Inverted Head and Shoulders pattern become complete.

The neckline of the Inverted Head and Shoulders pattern forms the resistance level. As soon as the resistance level is crossed, the bullish reversal occurs and the price starts to move upwards for the currency.

The figure below denotes the Inverted Head and Shoulders pattern.

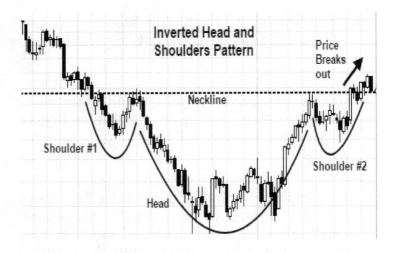

(Fig) Inverted Head and Shoulders Pattern

The chart depicts a currency that is in a downtrend. As soon as the Inverted Head and Shoulders pattern (also known as the Head and Shoulders bottom) is formed and the neckline is broken, it marks a change in the existing downtrend. The currency starts to form a bullish trend from then on.

Volumes: Volume has an important role in the Inverted Head and Shoulders pattern. During the formation of the first (left) shoulder, as well as the low of the head, the volume levels would be high. But during the formation of the low of the second (right) shoulder, the volume would be comparatively lower.

There would be an increase in volume during the advance from the low of the right shoulder to the neckline. After the second shoulder is also formed and the Inverted Head and Shoulders pattern is confirmed, the breakout from the neckline would happen at a very high volume.

Inverted Head and Shoulders pattern is one of the most reliable reversal patterns. Although it is ideal to have the two shoulders at the same level and symmetry, it is not mandatory. It is perfectly okay even if the height and/ or the width of the two shoulders are different.

Using the Inverted Head and Shoulders pattern, traders can choose new trades, identify stop loss levels of existing short positions, as well as plan target prices after taking long positions.

2.1.2.Rounding Bottom pattern

One of the dependable long-term reversal patterns is the Rounding Bottom pattern. It is also known as the **saucer bottom**. The Rounding Bottom pattern consists of a long period of price consolidation after which the trend changes from bearish to bullish. Hence, it is typically observed in weekly chart patterns.

How to identify a Rounding Bottom pattern?

When the price action of the currency happens in the following manner it is set to form a Rounding Bottom pattern.

The currency would be in a downtrend for a long period of time. Then it would decline further, creating a new low level. This low level formed would be the low of the Rounding Bottom and would take a few weeks to be completed.

After the low gets formed, the prices start to advance slowly. The right half of the pattern starts to be formed. Note that it takes almost the same time to form as the earlier decline of left half of the pattern.

Once the pattern reaches back to the reaction high from which the decline had started, a bullish confirmation is obtained. As soon as that happens, a breakout occurs and the prices start to soar.

The figure below shows the Rounding Bottom pattern.

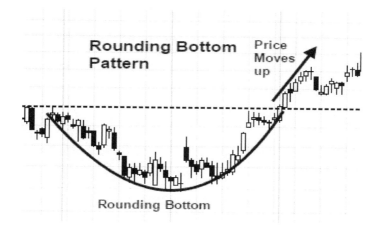

(Fig) Rounding Bottom Pattern

The chart above depicts a currency that was in a downtrend. As soon as the Rounding Bottom is formed and the price breakout happens, it marks the start of a bullish bias.

Volumes: The volume levels are usually high at the start of the decline and becomes lower towards the end of the decline (lowest point). During the advance, the volume level increases, especially during the price breakout.

Note that the Rounding Bottom pattern need not necessarily follow a smooth and linear pattern of decline and advancement. It can be formed in a jagged manner with lots of highs and lows. The left side and right side need not necessarily be symmetrical as well. The

185

important thing is to have the pattern's essence.

Using the Rounding Bottom pattern, traders can choose new longs, exit the short positions, as well as plan their target price and stop loss. This pattern is ideal for making decisions regarding the long-term position of the currency.

2.1.3. Double Bottom pattern

One of the prominent bullish reversal patterns is the Double Bottom pattern. This reversal pattern comprises of two almost identical troughs which are formed consecutively, with a peak in between them. The formation of this pattern indicates a trend reversal from bearish to bullish.

How to identify a Double Bottom pattern?

When the price action of the currency happens in the following manner, it forms a Double Bottom pattern.

There would be a significant downtrend of the market a few months before the pattern is formed. Then a trough will be formed which would be lower than the existing low of the downtrend. This is called as the first bottom.

186

After that, the price advances and forms a peak. This would be a resistance point which the price would not be able to cross. Then, the price declines further downwards and forms the second trough. It would take support at the earlier low formed by the first bottom. Then an advance in price occurs, reaching back to the earlier resistance level. Thus, the second bottom gets completed.

Once both the bottoms are formed, a price breaks out occurs and the trend starts to become bullish.

The figure below depicts a Double Bottom pattern.

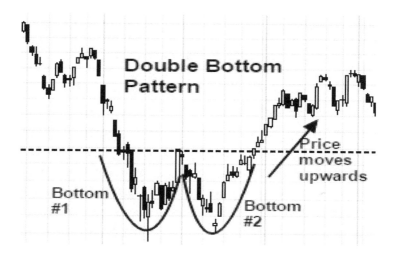

(Fig) Double Bottom Pattern

The chart above depicts a currency that is in a downtrend. As soon as the Double Bottom is formed and the price breakout happens, it marks the beginning of a bullish rally.

Volumes: The volume levels are usually low during the formation of the first bottom. Then there would be a slight increase in volume during the advancement to form the peak. The volume again decreases during the formation of the second bottom. During the advance from the second trough (bottom) to the neckline, the volume level increases. It is considerably higher when the price breakout occurs.

Using the Double Bottom pattern, traders can pick entry points for taking long positions, plan the exit points of the short positions, as well as pick their target price and stop loss.

2.1.4. Triple Bottom pattern

The Triple Bottom pattern is a bullish reversal pattern that consists of three nearly identical troughs which are formed consecutively, with a peak in between them. The formation of this pattern is a little difficult to identify. But once found, it is a powerful indicator that the trend is about to reverse from bearish to a bullish bias.

How to identify a Triple Bottom pattern?

A Triple Bottom pattern is formed during a downtrend. There would be three attempts done for pushing the price downwards through a support area. Each of these attempts would be characterized by the formation of a trough (bottom). This pattern actually indicates a fight for a balance between sellers and buyers, with the buyers eventually winning and reversing the trend to the bull market.

When the price action of the currency happens in the following manner, it forms a Triple Bottom pattern.

During a downtrend, a trough will be formed which would be lower than the existing low of the downtrend. This is called as the first bottom.

After that, the price advances and forms a peak. Then, the price declines further downwards and forms the second trough. This is the second bottom. It would take support at the earlier low formed by the first bottom.

Again, a price advance happens, forming another peak. After this, the price declines again and takes support at the earlier low, forming the third trough. This is the third bottom of the Triple Bottom pattern.

Once all three of the bottoms are formed, a price breaks out occurs from the neckline and the trend starts to become bullish.

The figure below depicts a Triple Bottom pattern.

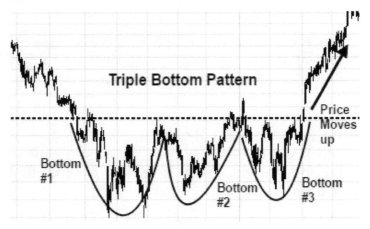

(Fig) Triple Bottom Pattern

The chart above depicts a currency that is in a downtrend. As soon as the Triple Bottom is formed and the price breakout happens, it marks the beginning of a bullish rally.

Volumes: The volume levels are usually low during the formation of the first, second, as well as third bottom. There would be a slight increase in volume during the advancement to form the peaks. During the advance from the final trough (third bottom) to the neckline, the volume level increases. The volume is significantly high when the price breakout occurs.

Traders use the Triple Bottom pattern for picking the entry points for long positions, exiting short positions, identifying the target price, as well as planning the stop loss levels.

2.2. Bearish Chart Patterns

After the price of the currency increases for some time, certain external factors could result in reversal of the price. This is reflected by the formation of bearish chart patterns.

Some of the important bearish chart patterns are Head and Shoulders formation, Double Top formation, Triple Top formation, and Rounding Top formation.

2.2.1. Head and Shoulders pattern

Head and Shoulders pattern is one of the most dependable patterns that predicts an imminent trend reversal from bullish to a bearish bias.

How to identify Head and Shoulders pattern?

When the price action of the currency happens in the following manner it is set to form a Head and Shoulders pattern.

After having a prolong bullish trend, the price starts to climb and form a peak and then suddenly goes down to create a trough. This becomes the first shoulder (left shoulder).

Soon after that, price increases again and forms a peak price which is higher than the maximum price of the left shoulder. After this, the price decreases again and creates another trough. This forms the Head.

Again, the price starts to climb up and form a third peak. But this peak would be only roughly as high as the first peak. Soon after, the price decreases again and comes back to the level of the first trough. This becomes the second shoulder (right shoulder).

An imaginary line connecting the first and second trough is called as a neckline. Once the Head and Shoulders pattern is confirmed, the bullish bias ends and a bearish trend starts.

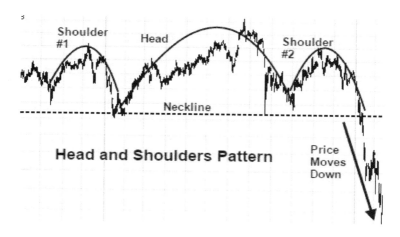

(Fig) Head and Shoulders Pattern

The chart depicts a currency that is in an uptrend. As soon as the Head and Shoulders pattern is formed and the neckline is broken, it marks a change in the existing uptrend. The currency starts to move downwards and reverse its trend from bullish to a bearish bias.

Volumes: Volume has an important role in the Head and Shoulders pattern. When forming the first (left) shoulder, as well as the top of the head, the volume levels would be high. But during the formation of the peak of the second (right) shoulder, the volume would be comparatively lower.

There would be an increase in volume when moving from the peak of the right shoulder downwards to the neckline. When the

193

breakdown happens from the neckline, the volume would be very high.

Head and Shoulders pattern is one of the most reliable reversal patterns. Although it is ideal to have the two shoulders at the same level and symmetry, it is not mandatory. It is perfectly okay even if the height and/ or the width of the two shoulders are different.

Using the Head and Shoulders pattern, traders can identify stop loss levels of existing long positions, choose short positions, as well as plan target prices after taking short positions.

2.2.2 Rounding Top pattern

Formation of Rounding Top pattern (also called as **Inverse Saucer**) usually occurs at the top end of a price uptrend in currency. This pattern signifies the reversal of market from bullish to a bearish trend.

How to identify a Rounding Top pattern?

When the price action of the currency happens in the following manner it is set to form a Rounding Top pattern.

The currency would be in an uptrend for a long period of time. Then the price would increase further, creating a new high. This high formed would be the highest point of the Rounding Top.

After the high gets formed, the prices start to decline slowly. The right half of the pattern starts to be formed.

Once the pattern reaches back to the reaction low from which the price increase had started, a bearish confirmation is obtained. As soon as that happens, a breakout occurs and the prices start to tumble down rapidly.

The figure below shows the Rounding Top pattern.

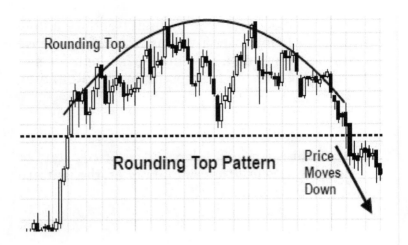

(Fig) Rounding Top Pattern

The chart above depicts a currency that was in an uptrend. As soon as the Rounding Top is formed and the price breakdown happens, it marks the start of a bearish market trend.

Volumes: The volume levels are usually high at the start of the price increase and becomes lower towards the highest point. During the decline, the volume level gradually increases and is highest during the price breakdown

Note that the Rounding Top pattern need not necessarily have a symmetrical left side and right side.

Using the Rounding Top pattern, traders can exit trades, pick new short positions, set a stop loss, and plan the target price as well.

2.2.3 Double Top pattern

The Double Top pattern is a bearish reversal pattern and is usually observed at the end of a bullish run.

How to identify a Double Top pattern?

When the price action of the currency happens in the following manner it is set to form a Double Top pattern.

There would be a significant uptrend of the market a few months before the Double Top pattern is formed. Then a new high in price would be formed. This is called as the first top.

After that, the price declines and forms a trough. This would be a support area from which the price would not fall further, and is called as the neckline. From there, the price moves upwards and forms the second peak. The peak would be formed at the same level as the first top. Then the price starts to decrease and heads back to the earlier neckline, forming the second top.

Once both the tops are formed, a price breaks down occurs and the trend starts to become bearish.

The figure below depicts a Double Top pattern.

(Fig) Double Top Pattern

The chart above depicts a currency that was in an uptrend. As soon as the Double Top pattern is formed and the price breakdown happens, it marks the beginning of a bearish trend.

Using the Double Top pattern, traders can pick entry points for taking short positions, plan the exit points of the long positions that are being held, as well as pick target price and set a stop loss.

2.2.4 Triple Top pattern

Triple Top patterns are rare bearish reversal patterns indicating the end of a bull run.

How to identify a Triple Top pattern?

When the price action of the currency happens in the following manner it is set to form a Triple Top pattern.

The currency would be in an uptrend before starting the formation of Triple Top pattern. First a new high in price would be formed in the uptrend. This is called as the first top.

After that, the price declines and forms a trough. This would be a support area from which the price would not fall further, and is called as the neckline. From there, the price moves upwards and forms the second peak. The peak would be formed at the same level as the first top. Then the price starts to decrease and heads back to the earlier neckline, completing the second top.

Again, the same pattern is repeated. Price increases and forms the third top and then decreases to reach the neckline.

Once all three tops are formed, a price breaks down occurs and the trend starts to become bearish.

The figure below depicts a Triple Top pattern.

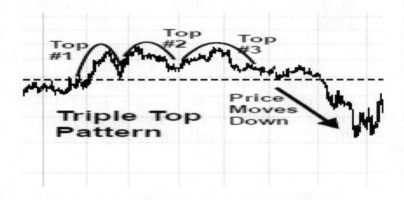

(Fig) Triple Top Pattern

The chart above depicts a currency that was in an uptrend. As soon as the Triple Top pattern is formed and the price breakdown happens, it marks the beginning of a bearish trend.

Using the Triple Top pattern, traders can select entry points for taking short positions, plan the exit of the long positions that are being held, as well as pick target price and set a stop-loss.

2.3 Continuation Chart Patterns

Whenever chart patterns like Flags, Bullish Rectangle, and Bullish Pennant are formed during an uptrend, they indicate that the prevalent uptrend would continue for a while. In the same vein, whenever chart patterns like Flags, Bearish Rectangle, and Bearish Pennant are formed during a downtrend, they indicate that the prevailing downtrend would continue for a while.

Hence, these patterns are called as continuation chart patterns. Following are some examples of continuation chart patterns.

2.3.1 Rectangle Pattern

The chart below shows the formation of a rectangle pattern during a price uptrend. A rectangle pattern basically acts as a consolidation phase before the next big move.

(Fig) Bullish rectangle Pattern

2.3.2 Flag Pattern

The chart below shows a flag pattern formed during a price uptrend. A flag pattern basically indicates that the price would continue to move upwards and the bullish trend would continue for a while.

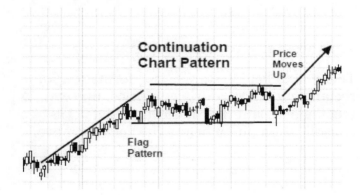

(Fig) Bullish flag Pattern

2.3.3 Triangle Pattern

The chart below shows an ascending triangle pattern being formed during a price uptrend. A triangle indicates that the price would continue to move in the upward direction.

(Fig) Ascending Triangle Pattern

3 Fibonacci Retracement

One of the highly useful indicators for Forex is the Fibonacci retracement. Fibonacci retracement helps in identifying the areas of support or resistance of the currency price.

Whenever there is a significant movement in price in the upwards or downwards direction, there is a support or resistance level created called Fibonacci retracement levels. These Fibonacci retracement levels are static and do not change.

How are Fibonacci retracement levels created?

For creating Fibonacci retracement levels, first, a trend line is drawn between the high and low prices. Then the vertical distance between the highest price and lowest price is divided into key Fibonacci ratios.

The Fibonacci ratios are 23.6%, 38.2%, 50%, 61.8% and 100%. Typically, a tool is provided in the charting software for automatically creating the Fibonacci levels. This can be best understood with the aid of an example shown below.

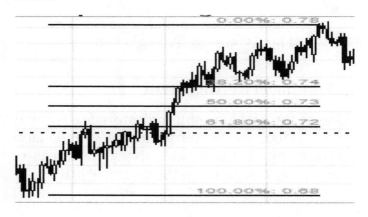

(Fig) Fibonacci Retracement Levels

The above chart shows a currency that is in an uptrend. Assume that the currency moved from 0.68 to 0.78. Then the various Fibonacci retracement levels are:

- 100% which is 0.68
- 61.8% which is 0.72
- 50% which is 0.73
- 38.2% which is 0.74
- 0% which is 0.78

From the above chart, the Fibonacci ratios can be used to identify the levels up to which the currency can correct. The levels marked in the chart would act as the support levels in case a correction happens in the next few days.

This means that the price can move down and take a support at the 38.2%, or 50%, or 61.8% levels before continuing the uptrend.

Using these Fibonacci levels, traders can take new trades, choose stop loss levels, as well as plan target prices for exiting the trades.

Chapter 3: Advanced Analysis of Forex

The price movements of Forex instruments are dependent on both fundamental as well as technical factors. As a forex trader, it is very important to have a good understanding of both fundamental and technical analysis in order to be successful.

1 Fundamental Factors

There are lots of fundamental factors that can impact the direction in which a currency moves. Anything that affects the economic or political strength of a country can be termed as a Fundamental factor. Following are the 6 major fundamental factors that affect the Forex market.

- *Political environment:* Any unrest in a country like a war or natural disaster can impact Forex. Political factors like raising taxes can also impact the country's currency. In order to have a stable currency, stability in the country is needed. This is because anything that affects the international trade of a country will affect the underlying currency of the country

- **_Trade Balance:_** Another important factor affecting the currency of a country is its trade balance. Countries that have a trade surplus will have basically a stronger currency. So what is a trade surplus? Trade surplus occurs when the amount export of goods from the country is greater than the import of goods into the country. Hence, trade surplus indicates a strong economy. Likewise, when there is a trade deficit, the currency of the country will get weaker. Trade deficit is when the imports are greater than the exports.

- **_GDP and Wealth:_** GDP or Gross Domestic Product is an economic indicator that indicates the health of a country's economy. GDP is nothing but the value of all the goods and services produced in a country over a period of time. A country with a strong and fast-growing GDP would have a stronger currency. The wealth of a country can be said as the sum of all its cash, gold and natural resources it holds. A wealthy country would have a better ability to pay off its loans and attract foreign investors. Hence such countries will have a stronger currency.

- **_Interest rates:_** The forex rate is influenced by the interest rate decisions made by the country's central bank. The Central bank holds periodic meetings to make decisions on the interest rates. The currency of a country is greatly influenced by these key decisions. Let us understand this with an example. If the 6-month interest rates of country A is 1 % lower than that of country B, and assuming all other things as equal, then there will be more demand for the currency of country B.

- *Inflation:* Inflation is another major factor that affects the currency of a country. The currency of countries with lower inflation will be more in demand than that of countries with higher inflation. Let us again try to understand with an example. If a country has an inflation of 12 % and the short term return in that country is 10 %, then it would not make much sense to invest in that country or in other words its currency.

- *Debt:* Economies with higher debts will find it hard to attract foreign investors. Also with high debt inflation will get bigger. All these would weaken the currency of a country. Having said this if the country has a lot of reserves (cash, gold or natural r resources), then the high debt might not always be a problem as the country would then have the ability to repay its loans. So it is important to see the overall economic strength of the country and not just the debt alone.

Apart from fundamental factors, speculation also plays a part in determining the movement of a currency. When the currency of a country is in demand, investors will demand more of that currency in order to make a profit in the short term. Thus the value of the currency will rise.

This basically means that when the demand is more than the supply the currency rises and when the supply is more than the demand the currency falls. Technical Analysis can be used to determine if the supply or the demand is more at a particular point in time.

2 Technical Factors

Forex Advanced Technical Analysis can be used for finding if Forex instrument is in a trend or in a range. The technical analysis is used to determine the supply and the demand for the Forex instrument at a particular point of time. The basis of technical analysis is speculation and crowd behavior. Technical analysis makes use of historical data to determine future price movements. Technical analysis consists of various tools and indicators that helps in this purpose. We will be discussing a few advanced technical analysis strategies in the next chapter.

Chapter 4: Advanced

Strategies of Forex

1 Advanced Forex strategy based on Divergence

Divergence is one of the advanced Forex strategies that gives a clear indication of trend changes that are about to occur. MACD - Price divergence occurs whenever the movement of price is not in sync with the movement of MACD. There are two types of divergences – Positive Divergence and Negative Divergence.

Trading Strategy: As soon as a positive divergence is seen, choose long positions in Forex. Whenever a negative divergence is seen, choose short positions in Forex.

This is best explained with the help of an example. The chart below shows the movement of price relative to the MACD line and MACD Histogram.

Case 1: Positive Divergence: As indicated in the chart of EUR/CAD below, the price made lower lows while the MACD Histogram started to climb and made higher lows. This is called as a positive divergence. After that, prices start to move upwards.

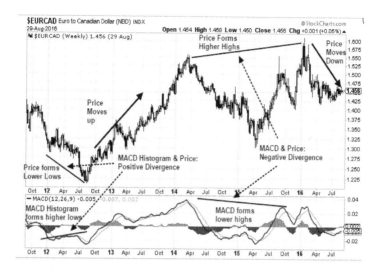

(Fig) Positive and Negative Divergence strategy

Case 2: Negative Divergence: As indicated in the chart of EUR/CAD above, the price made higher highs while the MACD line started to make lower highs. This is called as a negative divergence. After that, prices start to move downwards.

2 Advanced Forex strategy based on Fibonacci Retracements

One of the low-risk trading strategies for a currency that is in a trend is Fibonacci Retracement. During a trend, the currency corrects to a certain level before making the next move in the same direction. The various levels to which a correction or retracement occurs and takes support before continuing the trend is identified using the Fibonacci retracement levels.

Trading Strategy: In case the currency is in an uptrend, enter long positions whenever the price retrace downwards towards Fibonacci retracement levels of the upward movement.

If the currency is in a downtrend, enter short positions whenever prices retrace upwards towards the Fibonacci retracement levels of the downmove.

This is best explained with an example. The chart shows AUD/USD in an uptrend. The price moves from 0.68 to 0.78 as shown below. The various support levels are also identified and marked.

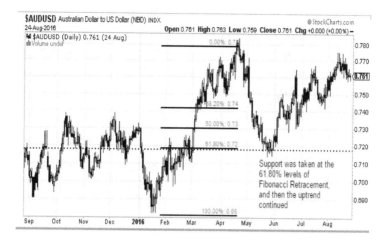

(Fig) Fibonacci Retracement Strategy

As observed from the chart, the price makes a retracement and takes support at the 61.8% Fibonacci retracement level before bouncing back to the earlier uptrend.

3 Advanced Forex strategy using combination of Bollinger Bands and Stochastics

Bollinger Bands basically identify the volatility of the currency. It consists of three bands – an upper band, a lower band, and a middle band which is a 20 SMA. The bands expand whenever the price is volatile and contract whenever they are stable. Stochastics are used for identifying whether the currency is in overbought or oversold levels. Bollinger Bands in conjunction with Stochastics gives a clear entry as well as exit signals for trades.

Trading Strategy: Enter long positions whenever the Stochastics is in oversold level (below 20) and the price is near the lower band of the Bollinger Bands.

Go for shorts whenever the Stochastics is in overbought level (above 80) and the price is near the upper band of the Bollinger Bands.

This is best explained with an example. As indicated in the chart of EUR/USD below, price moved above the top band of Bollinger bands. There was also a shooting star candlestick pattern indicating a bearish bias. At the same time, stochastics moved above 80, signifying an overbought level. This forms a good setup for entering into short positions. As you can see, soon afterward, price moved downwards.

(Fig) Bollinger Bands and Stochastics Strategy

For exiting the short position, wait until stochastics reaches to the oversold levels and the price moves down to reach the level of the lower band. When that happens, exit the short position.

4 Advanced Forex strategy based on chart patterns

Some of the important chart patterns were discussed in the earlier chapter on advanced concepts of Forex. The Forex trading strategy for each chart pattern and their target price is as follows:

I. Inverted Head and shoulders pattern

Trading Strategy: As soon as an inverted head and shoulders pattern is completed and breaks out from the resistance at the neckline, choose long positions for the currency. Exit the trade when the target price is reached.

Target Price: The target price for this move would be equal to the price at neckline + the price difference between the neckline and the lowest trough of the head.

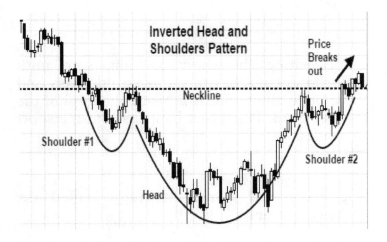

(Fig) Inverted Head and Shoulders Pattern

This is best explained with an example. Assume that the price at the neckline is 1.70 and the lowest price of the trough of the 'head' is 0.80. This means that the difference between the neckline and the lowest point of 'head' is 0.90. Then the target price of this Inverted Head and Shoulders pattern would be

1.70 (neckline's price) + 0.90 (price difference) = 2.60.

II.   Rounding Bottom pattern

Trading Strategy: As soon as the Rounding Bottom pattern is completed and breaks out from the resistance at the neckline, choose long positions for the currency. Exit the trade when the target price is reached.

Target Price: The target price for this move would be equal to the price at reaction high + the price difference between the reaction high and the lowest level of the Rounding Bottom.

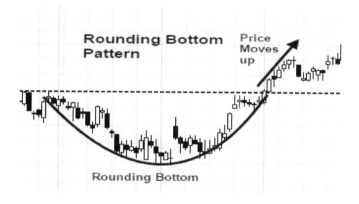

(Fig) Rounding Bottom Pattern

This is best explained with an example. Assume that the price at the reaction high is 1 and the lowest price of the Rounding Bottom is 0.30. This means that the difference between the reaction high and lowest point is 0.70. Then the target price of this Rounding Bottom pattern would be

217

1.0 (reaction high price) + 0.70 (price difference) = 1.70.

III.   Double Bottom pattern

Trading Strategy: As soon as the Double Bottom pattern is completed and breaks out from the resistance at the neckline, choose long positions for the currency. Exit the trade when the target price is reached.

Target Price: The target price for this move would be equal to the price at resistance level + the price difference between the resistance level and the lowest level of the troughs of the Double Bottom.

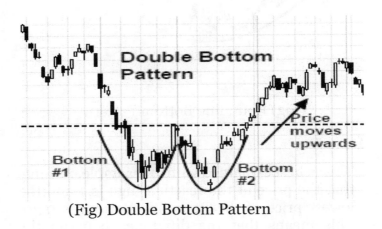

(Fig) Double Bottom Pattern

This is best explained with an example. Assume that the price at the neckline is 1.20 and the lowest price of the trough of the two bottoms is 0.80. This means that the difference between the neckline and the lowest point of the bottom is 0.40. Then the target price of this Double Bottom pattern would be

1.20 (neckline's price) + 0.40 (price difference) = 1.60.

IV.   Triple Bottom pattern

Trading Strategy: As soon as the Triple Bottom pattern is completed and breaks out from the resistance at the neckline, choose long positions for the currency. Exit the trade when the target price is reached.

Target Price: The target price for this move would be equal to the sum of the price at neckline + the price difference between the neckline and the lowest level of the troughs of the Triple Bottom.

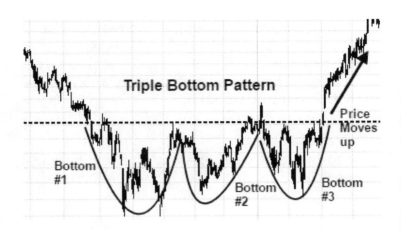

(Fig) Triple Bottom Pattern

This is best explained with an example. Assume that the price at the neckline is 0.90 and the lowest price of the trough of the three bottoms is 0.70. This means that the difference between the neckline and the lowest point of the bottom is 0.20. Then the target price of this Triple Bottom pattern would be

0.90 (neckline's price) + 0.20 (price difference) = 1.10.

V.   Head and shoulders pattern

Trading Strategy: As soon as the head and shoulders pattern is completed and breaks down from the support at the neckline, choose short positions for the currency. Exit the trade when the target price is reached.

Target Price: The target price for this move would be equal to the price at the neckline - the price difference between the neckline and the highest peak of the Head.

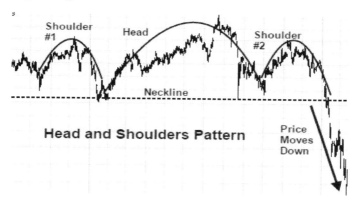

(Fig) Head and Shoulders Pattern

This is best explained with an example. Assume that the price at the neckline is 0.90 and the highest price of the peak of the 'head' is 1.20. This means that the difference between the neckline and the highest point of 'Head' is 0.30. Then the target price of this Head and Shoulders pattern would be

0.90 (neckline's price) - 0.30 (price difference) = 0.60.

VI.   Rounding Top pattern

Trading Strategy: As soon as the Rounding Top pattern is completed and breaks down from the support at the neckline, choose long positions for the currency. Exit the trade when the target price is reached.

Target Price: The target price for this move would be equal to the price at neckline – the price difference between the neckline and the highest level of Rounding top.

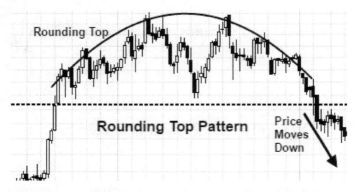

(Fig) Rounding Top Pattern

This is best explained with an example. Assume that the price at the neckline is 0.80 and the highest price of the Rounding Top is 1.10. This means that the difference between the neckline and highest point of Rounding Top is 0.30. Then the target price of this Rounding Top pattern would be

0.80 (price at neckline) - 0.30 (price difference) = 0.50.

VII.   Double Top pattern

Trading Strategy: As soon as the Double Top pattern is completed and breaks down from the support at the neckline, choose long positions for the currency. Exit the trade when the target price is reached.

Target Price: The target price for this move would be equal to the price at the neckline - the price difference between the neckline and the highest level of the peaks of the Double Top.

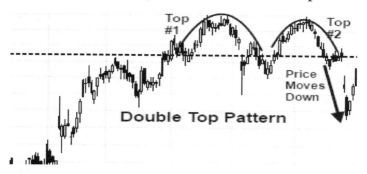

(Fig) Double Top Pattern

This is best explained with an example. Assume that the price at the neckline is 1.20 and the highest price of the peak of the two tops is 1.80. This means that the difference between the neckline and the highest point of the top is

0.60. Then the target price of this Double Top pattern would be

1.20 (neckline's price) - 0.60 (price difference) = 0.60.

VIII.   Triple Top pattern

Trading Strategy: As soon as the Triple Top pattern is completed and breaks down from the support at the neckline, choose long positions for the currency. Exit the trade when the target price is reached.

Target Price: The target price for this move would be equal to the price at the neckline - the price difference between the neckline and the highest level of the peaks of the Triple Top.

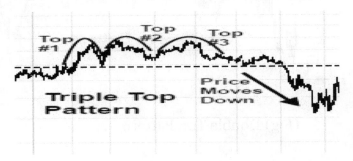

(Fig) Triple Top Pattern

This is best explained with an example. Assume that the price at the neckline is 1.10 and the highest price of the peak of the two tops is 1.40.

This means that the difference between the neckline and the highest point of the top is 0.30. Then the target price of this Triple Top pattern would be

1.10 (neckline's price) - 0.30 (price difference) = 0.80.

IX.   Rising Wedge chart pattern

A rising wedge chart pattern is a reversal pattern found during a bull market. This is identified by the unique movement of the currency price. The price would initially have a wide trading range but then starts sloping upwards into a narrow trading range.

Trading Strategy: Enter short positions whenever a rising wedge pattern is observed during an uptrend.

Target Price: The target price for the rising wedge pattern would be equal to the 38.2%, 50.0%, or 61.8% Fibonacci retracement levels of the price movement of the wedge; or the price at the previous low.

As indicated in the chart of USD/SGD below, price movements lead to the formation of a rising wedge pattern during the uptrend.

(Fig) Rising Wedge Pattern

As soon as the pattern was observed, the trend starts to reverse to a bearish bias and the price starts to move down.

X.   Flags

Trading Strategy: Enter short positions whenever a flag pattern is observed during a downtrend. Enter long positions whenever a flag pattern is observed during an uptrend.

Target Price: The target price for the flag pattern would be equal to the height of the flagpole. This is best explained with an example. Assume that the price at the bottom of the flagpole is 1.10 and the highest peak of the flagpole 1.40. This means that the height of the flagpole is 0.30. Then the target price of the Flag pattern would be

1.40 (price at top of flagpole) + 0.30 (height of flagpole) = 1.70.

As indicated in the chart of USD/SGD below, price movements lead to the formation of a flag pattern during the uptrend.

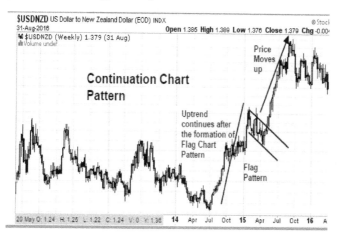

(Fig) Flag Pattern

As soon as the flag pattern was complete, price moved upwards up to the height of the flagpole.

XI.   Cup and Handle pattern

The cup and handle pattern is a bullish pattern. Ideally, the pattern would take a few weeks to months to form. The longer it takes to form, the more valid it is. Having said this, this pattern can also form in shorter time frames.

The pattern is an extension of the **Rounding Bottom** formation. After the cup is formed, the forex instrument then consolidates sideways for some time to form the handle. The breakout happens when the price breaks out of the neckline.

Trading Strategy: As soon as the Cup and Handle pattern is completed and breaks out from the resistance at the neckline, choose long positions for the currency. Exit the trade when the target price is reached.

Target Price: The target of this pattern can be calculated as (Highest point of the cup − Lowest point of the cup) + price at neckline. Please note that the target is an approximate target and you may exit the trade when supply sets in.

Given below is an example of Cup and Handle pattern formed on $USDSEK.

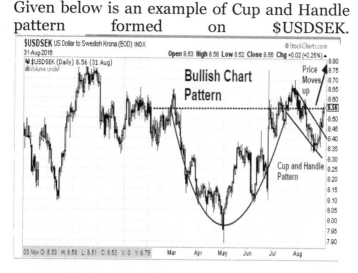

(Fig) Cup and Handle Pattern

The currency pair was in a downtrend and then consolidated to form the base of the cup. It then moved up to complete the cup or the rounding bottom pattern. It then consolidated sideways to form the handle. The breakout or the entry would be when the price breaks out of the neckline. The stop loss for such a trade would be a few pips below the low of the lowest point of the handle.

5 Advanced Trend Trading Strategy

Trend trading is one of the simplest forms of trading a forex instrument. When a Forex instrument trends, it forms a series of higher highs and higher lows if it's in an uptrend. Similarly, it forms a series of lower lows and lower highs if it's in a downtrend. There are mainly two basic methods of trading when the price is trending. They are Trend Line trading and buying on pullbacks. These strategies are used in conjunction with Stochastics for accurate entry and exit

(i) **Trendline Trading:** In case the Forex instrument is in an uptrend, draw a line joining two or more higher lows. This line is called a trend line and it now acts as a support. In the case of a downtrend, draw the line joining the lower highs and this line now acts as a resistance.

Trading Strategy: Let us take the example of $USDZAR to discuss the Trend Line trading strategy.

(Fig) Trendline Trading Strategy

As can be seen from the chart below $USDZAR is in an uptrend and is making a series of higher highs and higher lows. So a trend line can be drawn joining the higher lows. The **buy signal** would be when the price touches the trend line after a correction. When this happens, the stochastic would have to be in the **oversold** region too. The various buy signals are marked on the chart below. The **exit signal** would be when the price breaks below the trend line as shown in the chart below.

(ii) **Buying on pullbacks:** The second strategy of trading a trending forex instrument would be to buy on pullbacks or corrections to a moving average.

Trading Strategy: Let us take the example of USD/GBP to discuss the Trend Line trading strategy. When in an uptrend or downtrend the forex instrument would make periodic corrections or pullbacks. A buy signal would be triggered when the $USDGBP corrects to the 50 WMA as indicated in the chart below.

(Fig) Buying during pullbacks

6 Advanced Andrews pitchfork strategy

Andrews Pitchfork is a trading tool that is used when the market is trending. It consists of three lines that are equidistant from each other. Most charting software provides the Andrew Pitchfork tool. The important part about drawing Andrews Pitchfork is selecting the first 3 points.

1. **Point 1 :** Select the lowest point at the start of the trend
2. **Point 2:** Select the first Pivot high that is formed after the uptrend starts.
3. **Point 3:** Select the first Pivot low formed after Point 2.

Once these 3 points are marked, the Andrews Pitchfork tool automatically draws the three lines. Also, draw a line manually joining points 1 and 3.

Once the trend starts, the 3 lines act as support and resistance and can be used as entry and exit signals. The trend is said to be over when the price breaks below the line joined between 1 and 3.

Trading Strategy: Choose the entry point for long positions whenever the price is near the area of support. Choose short positions whenever the Forex instrument is near the area of resistance.

This is best explained with an example. In the chart of USD/GBP, Andrews Pitchfork is drawn using the 3 points.

As seen in the chart below, the three lines acted as support and resistance in a number of cases and can have been used as entry and exit points.

(Fig) Andrews Pitchfork Strategy

7 Advanced Forex strategy in a range-bound market

Trading in a range bound market is a little tricky. It is important to buy or sell at the correct point, or else you would end up at the wrong side of the trade. In a range bound market, the price would be fluctuating between two channels as is shown in the chart below.

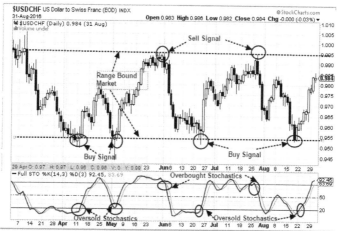

(Fig) Trading in a range bound market

Trading Strategy: Buy at the higher end of the channel and sell at the lower end of the channel. Stochastics can be used to get buy and sell signals when the price is in a range.

Buy Signal: is generated in following scenarios:

- Price touches the lower end of the channel
- Bullish reversal candle is formed (Doji, Hammer, Morning Star etc.)
- Stochastic is in the oversold region

Sell Signal: is generated in following scenarios:

- Price touches the upper end of the channel
- Bearish reversal candle is formed (Doji, Hanging man, Evening Star etc.)
- Stochastic is in the overbought region

The above example of USD/CHF shows that the price is in a range bound channel. Buy and Sell signals are marked on the chart based on the conditions listed above.

8 Advanced Forex strategy based on Momentum Indicators

Momentum indicators are highly useful for discerning the strength as well as weakness in a currency price. It basically measures the rate of fall or rise of the currency prices. This is done by comparing the current price of the currency with respect to past prices.

The calculation of momentum indicator is very simple. Assume that the number of periods selected is defined as 'n'. Then momentum indicator is equal to the current price minus the price before 'n' periods. For e.g, if the period selected is 12 days, then

Momentum indicator = current price – price before 12 days.

Trading Strategy: Momentum indicators can be used for identifying the buy as well as sell signals.

Buy Signal: Whenever the momentum indicator moves and crosses above the zero line, it indicates a bullish signal. Crossing above zero line indicates that price is reversing the course after bottoming out, or the price is moving and breaking above the recent highs.

Sell Signal: Whenever the momentum indicator moves and crosses below the zero line, it indicates a bearish signal. Crossing below zero line indicates that price is reversing the course after it had topped out, or the price has broken down below the recent low levels.

The chart below shows a practical example of the working of Momentum Indicator.

Whenever the indicator crosses below the zero line, a sell signal is triggered. If you note the corresponding price movement, you can see that the price moves downwards soon after the cross happens below the zero line.

(Fig) Trading Strategy based on Momentum Indicator

Similarly, whenever indicator crosses above the zero line, a buy signal is triggered. If you note the corresponding price movement, you can see that the price starts trending upwards soon after the cross happens above the zero line.

9 Advanced Forex strategy using Multi-time frame

The advanced strategy of ***Multi time frame analysis*** makes use of multi-time frames to make an entry and exit into a forex instrument. In this strategy, the main trend would be first determined using the higher time frame.

238

The entry is then made using a lower time frame. This strategy also makes use of Stochastics to determine if the Forex instrument is oversold or overbought. Although various combinations of multi-time frames can be used, the combination of weekly -daily timeframe is used here.

Trading Strategy: First, use the weekly chart to determine the direction of the trend. It can be any of the following scenarios:

- If the weekly chart is making higher highs and higher lows, then the trend is up and only long positions should be considered.
- If the weekly chart is making lower lows and lower highs, then the trend is down and only short positions should be considered.
- If the weekly chart is trading inside a range, then long positions should be considered only at the lower end of this range and short positions should be considered only at the upper end of this range.

Once the trend is decided based on the weekly time frame, an entry must then be made based on the daily charts.

- In case that the trend in the weekly chart is up. Then, a long position can be taken based on the daily chart centered on the following conditions.

1. A bullish reversal candle (doji, hammer, morning star etc.) is formed on the daily chart after a correction or a pullback to the 200 Daily Moving Average
2. Stochastic is in the oversold condition i.e. the stochastic is below 20

- In case the trend in the weekly is down, a short position can be taken based on the daily chart centered on the following conditions

1. A bearish reversal candle (doji, hanging man, evening star etc.) is formed on the daily chart after a correction or a pullback to the 200 Daily Moving Average
2. Stochastic is in the overbought condition i.e. the stochastic is above 80.

- If the weekly chart is in a range, then

1. A Long position should be taken when the price is at the lower end of the range, and if there is a bullish reversal candle on the daily chart. The stochastic should also be oversold on the daily chart.
2. A Short position should be taken only when the price is at the upper end of the range and there is a bearish reversal candle on the daily chart. In this case,

the stochastic should be in the overbought condition on the daily chart.

Let us understand this forex strategy with an example.

USD/MXN-Weekly and Daily

Based on the weekly chart of $USDMXN, it is quite evident that the currency pair is making a series of higher highs and higher lows and that the trend is up. So only long positions should be considered for the instrument.

(Fig) Identify trend using weekly chart

Now the buy signal or the entry for this trade should be done using the daily charts. The buy points are marked on the daily chart below.

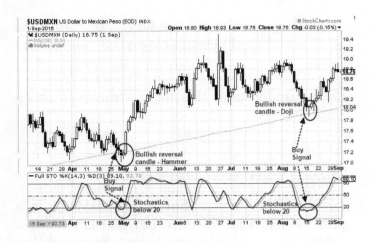

(Fig) Identify buy and sell signals using daily chart

A long position is taken when the currency pair corrects to the 200 DMA and a bullish reversal candle is formed. The stochastic should be in the oversold condition as well.

The sell signal for this particular trade is when the stochastic moves into the overbought region i.e. above 80.

Please note that any combination of the time frames can be used for this strategy. The above-mentioned combination of Daily and Weekly is more suitable for *swing traders* who are willing to hold the trade for a few days to weeks.

Traders who are interested in holding the trade only for a short duration should go for smaller time frames. A few commonly used combinations are **Daily and Hourly, Hourly and 15 minutes** and **15 minutes and 5 minutes**.

Also while using the shorter time frames a smaller moving average can be used instead of the 200-day moving average that we used in our example.

10 Advanced Forex strategy using ADX lines

ADX lines are used to determine the strength of a trend. ADX lines consist of the ADX line, the +DI line and the −DI line. This indicator is used mostly when the market is trending.

When the ADX line is above 20, the instrument is said to be trending. As the trend gets stronger, the ADX line keeps rising. Now lets us discuss an advanced forex strategy using the ADX line. Remember that the direction of the trend cannot be determined using this strategy. So trend direction should be first determined using any other strategy that we have already discussed.

Trading Strategy: By using ADX lines, entry, as well as exit criteria for a trade, can be determined. The ***entry*** conditions using this strategy are as follows.

- The +DI line should cross the -DI line to the upside
- The ADX line should cross 25

The ***exit*** signal is triggered when the ADX goes below 20. When the ADX goes below 20, it indicates that the trend is getting weaker. Anything below 20 indicates that the market is consolidating or trading in a range.

Let us try to understand this strategy with an example using the $USDMXN-Weekly chart. After we have determined that we want to go long on this currency pair using some other strategy, we can take an entry into this instrument using the ADX lines. This helps us to buy into a strong trend.

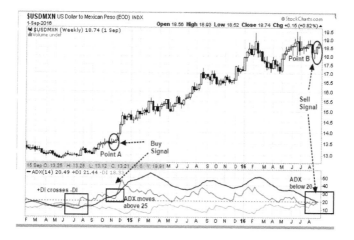

(Fig) ADX Lines Strategy

Based on our conditions mentioned above, we would have been able to make a long entry into this instrument at point A (marked on the chart). This exit signal is when the ADX goes below 20. So point B (market on the chart) is our exit point. So as you can see we were able to hold the currency pair when the trend was really strong and the exit it when the trend got weaker.

Bonus Chapter: How to become a successful Forex Trader? – Expert Tips

Following are a list of things required for becoming a successful Forex trader

1. *Trading plan:* A forex trader should have a trading plan that should be prepared well in advance. The trading plan should list out his entry and exit conditions as well as his money management rules. This is of utmost importance and he should religiously follow his trading plan to the tee. In order to become a successful forex trader, he should never deviate from the trading plan.

2. *Discipline:* This is one of the most important qualities needed to be a successful forex trader. A trader should be disciplined and methodical in the way he goes about with forex trading. He should not only meticulously plan his trading, but should also be disciplined enough to follow it.

3. *Ability to do analysis:* A forex trader should have the ability to analyze the technical charts and other financial

data in order to become a successful forex trader. He should invest in himself and learn how to use the financial tools that would help in becoming a better trader. Trading is a very competitive job and one needs to be always one step ahead of others in order to be successful.

4. ***Emotional stability:*** It is very important to keep emotions and trading separate. In order to be successful, the trader should be able to trade like a machine and not let emotions affect his trades. He shouldn't let losses affect him nor should he get overly excited about the winning trades.

5. ***Hard work:*** Nothing beats hard work for becoming a successful forex trader. The trader should be prepared to put in a lot of hours and research the forex market thoroughly before each trading day. Most successful forex traders have a pre-trading session wherein they analyze the global markets, check charts, read various financial newspapers, note down key economic events of the day etc. before they start their trades.

6. ***Good knowledge of charting and analysis tools:*** In order to be a successful forex trader, it is very important to have good knowledge on the usage of charting and other analytic software. The usage of these trading software's raises the odds of success

considerably, so it is important to have a good understanding of them.

7. **Constant Learning:** Trading field requires constant learning. The trader should be prepared to learn throughout his trading career. Something that might work now might not work after 5 years. So it's very important to constantly adapt and keep learning in order to be a step ahead of others. A good trader should be on the constant look out of learning new things that might help him with his trading be it the usage of a trading software or a new way of analysis.

8. **Mastering fear:** It is very important to master fear in order to be a successful forex trader. The trader should be prepared to take losses now and again and should understand that it's a part and parcel of the game. The inability to book losses and holding on to a losing position can result in more losses. The trader should also be ready to take a trade when a good opportunity arises and should not allow fear to hold him back.

9. **Thinking on your own:** It is very important to think on your own and make trading decisions and to not just blindly follow the crowd. As the saying goes, "buy into the fear and sell into the greed!" Now, this does not mean to

always do the opposite to what others do. It just means that the trader should have an open mind and should have the ability to think on his own and make decisions accordingly.

10. *Awareness of the global events:* Forex markets are affected by the major international events that occur. So it's important to have an understanding of the key economic events happening globally as the forex markets are traded globally and affected by these economic events. A few examples of the key economic events are Federal Bank interest rate decision, ECB rate decision, GDP data of key economies, job data of key economies, inflation data of key economies etc.

11. *Never blame the market:* The market might behave irrationally but the trader should be responsible for reading the market cues and making trading decisions. Instead of playing the blame game he should learn from each mistake and learn from it. The trader should understand the risks associated with trading and have a proper money management rule in place.

12. *Trading journal:* It is important to maintain a trading journal and make an entry of all the trades he makes. The reasons for taking that particular trade should also be noted down. This would

help in analyzing the trades later and help in avoiding the mistakes made. This would also help in identifying the good trades made and look for similar patterns later on.

13. ***Choosing the right broker:*** It is important to choose the right broker. Some of the factors that should be considered while selecting a broker should be a) low brokerage b) fast and reliable trading terminal c) ease of trading and good research and charting software's that the broker provides.

14. ***Money management rules:*** This is perhaps the most important among all things that are mentioned till now. A money management rule is basically the rules that define the maximum loss a trader can afford to take per trade or at a point of time. Most forex traders never risk more than 2- 5 % per trade. They also never risk more than 10-20 % at a particular point across all trades. It is very important to follow these rules; else you run the risk of wiping out your entire trading account in a matter of days, if not hours! It is always better to limit your losses and live to fight another day!

Conclusion

Thank you again for buying this book!

I hope this book was able to help you to understand the nuances of advanced concepts of Forex Trading, as well as the advanced Forex strategies in order to make profits from Forex market.

The next step is to follow the strategies and tips explained in the book and set your course towards financial freedom!

Thank you and good luck!

Jordon Sykes

Penny Stocks

Powerful Advanced Guide to dominate Penny Stocks

INTRODUCTION

I want to thank you and congratulate you for downloading the book, *"Powerful Advanced Guide to dominate Penny Stocks"*.

This book contains powerful steps and strategies on how to become an expert in Penny Stock trading. It holds some of the best-kept insider secrets and strategies for picking out Penny Stock winners, thereby getting you closer to your financial goals.

Various complex strategies and concepts pertaining to Penny Stocks are explained in a simple, easy to follow manner in this book. Supported with ample illustrations, charts, and actual examples, this book is guaranteed to bring in a paradigm shift in your understanding about Penny Stocks.

Within these pages, you will find

- Precisely what a Penny Stock means and where to trade them
- The importance of brokers and how their commissions can impact your profits – also how to avoid paying huge broker commissions.

- Why picking a good stock screener is vital.
- Various Penny Stock trading strategies
- Concepts about chart reading – candlestick patterns, chart patterns, volume analysis, and technical indicators
- Expert criteria for entering and exiting stocks
- Numerous Tips and Tricks to figure out Penny Stock winners

You will also learn...

How to limit your losses and increase your profit margins

The criteria for selecting a broker that suit your trading style

Secrets of successful Penny Stock trading

And lots more...

Remember, people spend THOUSANDS on courses to learn even a tenth of what is being disclosed in this advanced book on Penny Stock strategies.

You get the perfect solution by reading this book –learn how to get the top results with the slightest possible effort!

Thanks again for downloading this book, I hope you enjoy it!

CHAPTER 1: BRIEF INTRODUCTION TO PENNY STOCKS

"Here's the next big Penny Stock about to breakout – grab it before it is too late!"

"Top secret –hottest trending Penny Stocks"

"Double your money in a day using XYZ Penny Stocks"

Sounds familiar? These are just a few samples of promotions related to Penny Stocks found in magazines and newspapers. Chances are also high that you would notice numerous pop-ups of Penny Stock recommendations when browsing the internet.

The term 'Penny Stock' is exceedingly familiar to all. But not many comprehend the inner workings of it. This advanced guide on Penny Stocks covers all aspects of Penny Stocks: the various advantages and risks associated with Penny Stocks, tips to pick out Penny Stock winners, various useful tools, and resources, as well as advanced strategies for entering and exiting trades. So, let's get started right from the basics.

What is a Penny Stock?

Penny Stocks, also known as *micro-cap stocks* are simply the shares of a company that trades at very low prices.

Here are a few quick facts about Penny Stocks:

Price of a Penny Stock vary from fractions of a penny, or a penny; to a maximum of $5

Traders typically choose $1 as the standard for defining Penny Stocks.

Penny Stocks have very low market capitalization (hence, called micro-caps)

Although spread across all industries, the majority of Penny Stocks are concentrated in Resources, Medical/ Biotech products, and Technology sector.

Types of Penny Stocks

For the sake of convenience, Penny Stocks can be broadly divided into two categories.

Category 1: Stocks of small companies, or that of companies that were started recently.

Category 2: Stocks of older and reputable companies which used to trade above $5, but are currently trading below $5.

Where are Penny Stocks traded?

The Penny Stocks of the **first category** are normally quoted over the counter like

OTC Bulletin Board, also known as OTCBB

OTC Link LLC, also known as Pink OTC Markets Inc.

OTCBB

OTC Bulletin Board is an electronic quoting system that is used for buying as well as selling stocks outside of a formal exchange.

OTCBB is a facility of FINRA and combines the quotes from various brokers and market makers across electronic communication networks into one location.

OTC Link LLC

OTC Link LLC or Pink OTC Markets are also similar to OTCBB. They are operated by OTC Markets Group.

They have three tiers depending on the decreasing amount of regulation: OTCQX, OTCQB, and OTC Pink.

The chart below shows a quick summary.

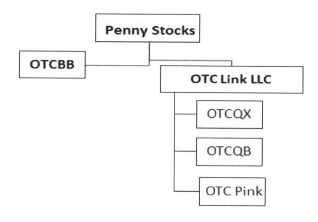

(Fig) Trading of Penny Stocks of Category #1

OTCQX: It is also known as the **Best Marketplace**.

OTCQX is basically for recognized investor-focused U.S. as well as international companies.

In order to be eligible for the OTCQX marketplace, companies should

Have high financial standards

Exhibit acquiescence with U.S. securities laws

Be up-to-date in their disclosure

Be supported by a professional third-party advisor.

OTCQB: It is also known as the ***Venture Marketplace***.

OTCQB is basically for U.S. as well as international companies which are in a developmental stage and incapable of qualifying for OTCQX.

In order to be eligible for the OTCQB marketplace, companies should

Be up to date current in their reporting

Go through a verification annually

Undergo a management certification process.

Not be in bankruptcy.

Pass a minimum $0.01 bid price test.

OTC Pink: It is also known as the ***Open Marketplace***.

OTC Pink allows trading through any broker, as well as the trading across a wide variety of equity securities.

There are no eligibility criteria as such for qualifying for OTC Pink. It allows any type of companies – be they in distress, default or even by design.

The Penny Stocks of the **second category** are traded on exchanges like

NYSE

NASDAQ

AMEX etc.

Although the cheap stocks listed on exchanges like NYSE and NASDAQ aren't technically "Penny Stocks", they bring in a lot of the benefits of Penny Stocks without too much risk, since they are all reputable companies.

Advantages of investing in Penny Stocks

Following are some of the advantages provided by Penny Stocks when compared to regular stocks.

#1 High reward ratio: The stock price of Penny Stocks are very low. This means that you can purchase a large amount of Penny Stocks using a fairly small amount of money, leading to higher profits. This is best understood using an example.

Assume that Person 'A' and Person 'B' each has $500 available to invest.

Person 'A' invests in a good Penny Stock which cost $0.10 per stock. On the other hand, Person 'B' invests in a regular stock that cost $20.0 per stock.

The table below shows the profits earned when each sells their stocks for two different hypothetical sell prices. You can see that the profits grow exponentially in the case of Penny Stocks.

Remember that the initial investment amount was same for both Person 'A' as well as Person 'B'. So, what exactly caused this big difference in profits?

Name	Type of Stock	Buy Price	# stocks	Sell Price	Profit Earned	Sell Price2	Profit Earned2
Person A	Penny Stock	$0.10	5000	$0.50	$2,000.00	$1.00	$4,500.00
Person B	Regular Stock	$20.00	25	$40	$500.00	$60	$1,000.00

(Fig) Understanding Reward Ratios of Penny Stocks

The answer lies in the number of shares purchased using the same $500. Person 'A' managed to buy 5000 shares while Person 'B' could purchase just 25 shares using the $500.

This means that for each price move, the profit earned by Person 'A' is a multiple of 5000 shares, while in the case of Person 'B', the price is multiplied by just 25!

dAs you observed, the growth potential of Good Penny Stocks is of an exponential nature. This means that it is possible to make double, triple, quadruple or even more times your investment amount using Penny Stocks within a few weeks to a year.

Penny Stocks thus provides the prospects of strong earnings for traders or investors who carefully enter and exit at the right time.

#2 Possibility of discovering hidden gems: Amongst the Penny Stocks that are listed on OTCBB and OTC Pink, there would be qualified, hardworking companies with very high growth potential. Identifying such companies would result in gaining a high amount of profits as the business ethics as well as management of such companies would be quite sound.

#3 Good learning opportunity for Novice investors: People new to investing can get the feel of the market by investing in Penny Stocks. Doing so will help them grasp the ins and outs pertaining to trading and investing without risking a huge chunk of money. Trading with Penny Stocks would give the novice investors the necessary confidence to trade in stock markets, rather than just demo accounts.

Risks involved in investing in Penny Stocks

Although the lure of the high rewards makes Penny Stocks irresistible, there are also things that warrant caution. Following are some of the risks associated with Penny Stocks. As the saying goes - Forewarned is forearmed!

#1 No clear standards: There are no well-defined standards available for Penny Stocks when compared to other regular stocks. This makes it riskier when compared to investing in regular stocks.

#2 Poor stability: The companies of Penny Stocks *can be closed* without any previous warning at any point in time, causing the buyers to lose money. This lack of stability is yet another risk associated with Penny Stocks.

#3 Unavailability of company information: It is not mandatory for the companies listed in OTC and Pink sheets to issue financial statements. Many of the companies have *no reportable history* as well. As it is not required for the companies to list their assets, the company could be a shell company or a bankrupt one and you wouldn't be aware of it. Hence, the risks associated with buying the Penny Stocks of the company is higher.

#4 Lack of liquidity: When compared to regular stocks, the number of trades done for Penny Stocks are usually lesser. Hence, it would be difficult to easily buy and sell Penny Stocks, as there are a lesser number of sellers and buyers. This is called as the lack of liquidity.

In addition, due to the *low frequency of trading*, it would be difficult to price the Penny Stocks with accuracy. Hence, Penny Stocks are also considered to be *speculative investments*. All these are risks associated with Penny Stocks.

#5 High probability of fraud: Due to the lack of regulations by SEC, Penny Stocks have a higher probability of occurrence of *scams* and swindling schemes.

Now that the basics have been refreshed, let us move on to the advanced concepts of Penny Stocks.

CHAPTER 2: PENNY STOCKS –

ADVANCED CONCEPTS

Importance of selecting a good broker

One of the most important aspects of Penny Stock trading – which is almost as crucial as the selection of stocks – is picking out the right broker. This is because the commission paid to a broker can literally break or make your trade. Unfortunately, not many pay heed to this aspect of trading and end up losing a good chunk of money by paying too much broker commissions.

So, what exactly does a broker do? Here's a quick rundown.

Brokers basically act as an intermediator between sellers and buyers.

A broker can be a person or a company who executes the buy or sell orders of the investor for a commission.

The services of a broker also include advice, deliveries, and negotiations.

Types of Penny Stock Brokers

Brokers of Penny Stocks are divided into two categories - Full-service Brokers and Discount brokers.

#1 Full-service Brokers

Following are the services provided by Full-service brokers:

Provide advice

Analyze market trends

Make predictions

Tax preparation

Provide tax tips

Real estate planning

Retirement planning

The drawback of full-service brokers is that they are very *expensive*. Full-service brokers have the highest commission rate −up to even $100 per trade. Full-service brokers provide a small discount for orders placed online.

Full-service brokers are *best suited for* people having a *complex financial* situation and are also too busy to stay updated on various issues pertaining to their finances.

#2 Discount brokers

Discount brokers are usually called as ***online brokers*** as they interact with the customers only over the internet, and not face to face at their office location

Following are the characteristics of discount brokers.

Discount brokers have a lower broker commission when compared to full-service brokers.

They do not provide advice or analysis.

They charge a lower amount for orders that are placed online.

The services provided are limited to just buying and selling orders at a lower commission

They do not provide investment services, personalized advice, and tax tips

Discount brokers are ***best suited for*** investors who prefer to do their own research. It is also best for ***active traders*** due to their low commission.

How much does the commission rate of a broker cost? Here are some quick facts about broker commission.

The commission rate of a broker depends on following factors

The price of the shares that are being traded

The category of underlying security

The frequency of trades made

The size of an investor's portfolio

Brokers charge an extra commission when trading Penny Stocks. More than 70% of brokers will have either hidden charges or higher commission rates for trading Penny Stocks.

The commission rates of different brokers can differ significantly. But the average cost per trade is on an average $7.25 for online brokers. Below are the commission rates of some of the popular brokers

TradeKing - $4.95 per trade

Sharebuilder - $6.95 per trade

Scottrade - $7 per trade

SureTrader - $4.95 per trade up to 1000 shares.

Charles Schwab - $8.95 per trade

ChoiceTrade - $7 per trade

TDAmeritrade - $9.99 per trade

OptionsXpress - $8.95 per trade

Types of Brokerage accounts

For Penny Stocks, there are mainly two types of brokerage accounts - Cash Account and Margin Account.

#1 Cash Account

1. Cash account is also called as Type 1 account.

2. This is the ***traditional*** brokerage account.

3. The entire cost of the purchase must be deposited by the time of the settlement date.

#2 Margin Account

☐ Margin account provides the flexibility to **borrow cash** for purchasing stocks using the securities or cash already available in the account as a collateral.

☐ If losses are incurred, the broker has the **right to sell** the stocks placed as collaterals to regain the money.

☐ For this reason, margin accounts are not recommended for newbies.

Criteria for selecting a Penny Stock Broker

Following are some of the important factors to be considered when selecting a broker for trading Penny Stocks.

- **Broker charges:** Check the charges per transaction for the broker. At times, the broker fees shown are valid only for the first month and could charge a higher rate in the later months.

There might also be minimum trading requirements like say, 30 trades a month for availing the lower fees. Always read the fine print before signing the dotted line.

- **Restrictions on trading**: Some brokers do not allow the short selling of Penny Stocks. The brokers who do allow these may have a higher margin requirement or would need additional margins. Check for these factors before picking out the broker.

- **Extra charges:** Brokers would have additional fees like annual maintenance fees, as well as charges for making money transfers. There might also be charges in the case of account inactivity, or for withdrawing money to bank accounts.

A yearly IRA fees would be charged for the ones with retirement accounts. There might also be volume limits and Surcharges for large orders. All these should be weighed in carefully before choosing the broker.

- **Response time:** The phone lines of some brokers would either be busy, or they would never pick up. Some brokers are hence difficult to get ahold of, especially if you need to make a transaction at a specific price or time. Hence it is best to choose a broker who is easily accessible.

- **Tools and Software:** An investor is only as good as his tool. It is best to choose brokers with robust trading platforms, mobile apps available for trading on the go, real time streaming of quotes, and other trading tools.

- **Market Researches**: Many brokers provide free market research as part of their service.

- **Security:** Before choosing a broker, check for their SSL websites and added security features like double verification and security questions. It is always best to go with a broker who is a member of FINRA and SIPC.

How to reduce broker fees: Pro Tips

Paying Broker Commissions can figuratively eat away most of your profits. In case you have a successful trade, the broker fees are deducted from the profits. On the other hand, in case your trade was unsuccessful, you would still need to shell out money for paying the broker in addition to the losses incurred.

But do not be disheartened, for there are ways to reduce paying a high fee to your broker. Here are some top tips to follow for saving money on broker commission.

#1 Avoid too much trading: Do not trade in an obsessive fashion. Always remember that every trade costs money. So, it is best to avoid trading strategies that require too much trading activities (buying and selling multiple times)

#2 Adjust your trading budget so that it includes money for brokerage: Always plan for the exit price of the trade by factoring in the money necessary to cover the broker commission. For instance, if your trade costs $10 in brokerage, exit the trade for at least a $15 profit.

Similarly, set your stop loss too with the broker fees (e.g. $10) in mind. If you intend to set $35 as a maximum loss in a trade, exit the trade when the actual loss reaches $25.

#3 Change your broker: Your trading style typically evolves over time. Sometimes, your existing broker might not be providing the best commission for the trading style you have currently adopted. So it is always a good practice to check and reevaluate your existing broker once in a while.

#4 Select simple trading strategies: Always choose the trading strategies that has the least amount of broker commission for every dollar invested. This means that it is best to avoid strategies like double-wide calendar spread!

#5 Avoid deceitful brokers: Despite the regulations set up by National Association of Securities Dealers (NASD) and SEC, there are brokers who deceive investors using unscrupulous practices. In case you find such brokers, it is best to avoid taking up their service.

Below are some of the ways by which these brokers commit fraud. Understanding them would help in avoiding these pitfalls

- ***Churning:*** The misuse of the discretionary authority of brokers over user accounts, in order to increase the broker commission through overtrading is called as churning.

How to identify it? Check for an excessive number of transactions in your trading account, without causing much change in your portfolio's value.

How to avoid it? Use a wrap account to avoid churning.

- **Withholding useful information**: Some unscrupulous brokers withhold beneficial information from investors for increasing their commissions. For instance, take the case of non-sharing of breakpoints with the investors.

This is best explained with an example.

Assume that your total investment amount is $3100. Now, if a mutual fund charges 7% for investing any amount less than $3000, and 4% if the investment amount is above $3000, than the threshold amount of $3000 is called as a breakpoint.

This means that investing the entire $3100 in one mutual fund would give you a lower charge.

Now, unethical brokers would distribute your $3100 investment in two similar mutual funds in order to earn commissions from both, while cheating you from the benefits of breakpoints.

In order to avoid it, the investor must keep up with the latest announcements and updates in order to stay ahead in the game.

- ***Doing transactions that are damaging to the investor:*** Every investor would have a list of do's and dont's to be followed emphatically. But some brokers do not follow these directions.

For instance, brokers can choose a high-risk trade when the investor is 100% risk averse.

At times, the broker might invest all money into one stock when the investor prefers a diversified portfolio.

If any of this sounds like your existing broker, it's time to reevaluate!

The broker commissions would not be too high if you do your research well. If you are using brokers in order to manage highly complex investments, there is no getting around their ridiculous fees. But in case you intend to do most of the research, and do the buying and selling on your own, your broker fees can be brought down to a huge extent.

Important Candlestick Patterns

The candlestick patterns play a very important role in trading the Penny Stocks. Here is a quick overview about candlesticks.

Every candlestick has four important parts – open price, close price, high price, and low price. The lines available at the ends of a candle are called as shadows.

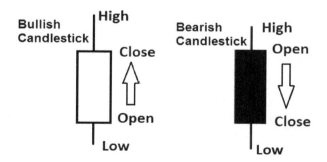

(Fig) Bullish and Bearish Candlesticks

The figure above represents bearish and bullish candlestick. White colored or empty candlesticks mean that the closing price was higher than the opening price. It is called as a bullish candlestick.

On the other hand, a filled, black, or red candlestick is a bearish candlestick. The closing price would be lesser than the opening price for a bearish candlestick.

In addition to Bullish and Bearish candlestick, there is also a neutral candlestick pattern called as Doji.

(Fig) Doji – Neutral Candlestick

Dojis are formed when the opening, as well as closing price of the stock, is same for the day. It can look like an inverted cross, cross, or a positive sign. Dojis usually represent an indecision in market direction.

A single candlestick or a combination of two or more candlesticks can be used to identify the bullish or bearish signals for the stock. Thus, candlestick charts can undeniably provide an edge in picking out winning trades. Next, let us examine some of the important bullish and bearish candlestick patterns

Bullish Candlestick patterns

The candlestick patterns that indicate a bullish bias for the market is called as Bullish candlestick patterns.

These patterns can be used for identifying good entry points for a trade. More details about the trading strategy would be explained in the later chapter on Advanced Buy Strategies for Penny Stocks.

Following are some of the important bullish candlestick patterns:

- Hammer

- Bullish Engulfing

- Piercing Line

- Morning Star

283

- Three White Soldiers

- Bullish Harami/ Harami Cross

- Bullish Belt Hold

- Bullish abandoned baby

#1 Hammer: Hammer is a single candlestick  pattern typically formed at the end of a bear run, indicating a trend change to Bullish bias. This candlestick will have a long lower shadow, and have a closing at the high price of the day (or nearer to it).

#2 Bullish Engulfing: Bullish engulfing 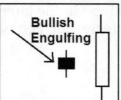 candlestick pattern consists of two candlesticks. The first candle would be a small black candle and it would be followed by a big white candle that would completely engulf the black candle. This pattern usually appears during a downtrend.

#3 Piercing Line: Piercing Line candlestick pattern is made of two candlesticks and is a bottom formation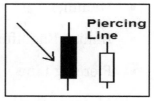

reversal pattern.

On the first day, a long black candle is formed. On the second day, a white candle is formed whose open price is lower than the close price of first day's candle.

The closing price of the second candle would be within the first day's candle.

Traders pick this pattern and draw a piercing line which cuts through both the candlesticks. Then they enter long positions with a stop loss set to be below the piercing line.

#4 Morning Star: Morning Star candlestick pattern is made of three candlesticks. The first day's candle would be a

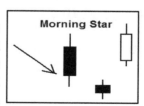

285

long black candle.

The second candle would be a small candlestick (white or black). The second candle would start by gaping below the close of the first day's candle. The third candles would be a long white one.

This pattern is helpful in identifying trend changes from bearish to a bullish bias.

#5 Bullish Belt Hold: Bullish Belt Hold candlestick pattern consists of just one

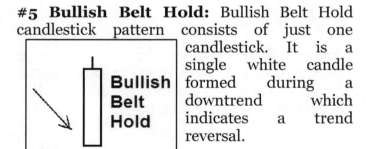

candlestick. It is a single white candle formed during a downtrend which indicates a trend reversal.

The low of the candlestick would be its open price and there would be a price rally during the day, resulting in the closing of the candlestick at the high or very near the high.

A small shadow could be formed at the top of the candle, but not at the bottom.

The strength of reversal depends on the length of the candle's body – longer the body, stronger the reversal!

#6: Bullish Harami, Bullish Harami 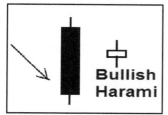 **Cross**: Bullish Harami as well as Bullish Harami Cross are bullish reversal patterns that are made of two candlesticks.

In Bullish Harami Pattern, the first candle would be a black candle.

The second candle would be a white candle that would have a small body. This second candle would be completely within the range of the first candlestick's body.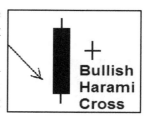

287

In the case of Bullish Harami Cross pattern, there is just one minor difference – the second candlestick would be a doji.

#7 Bullish Abandoned Baby: Bullish Abandoned baby pattern indicates a major bottom reversal and is formed during a downtrend. It consists of three candlesticks.

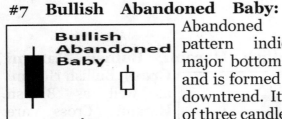

The first candle would be a black candle.

The second candle would be a Doji. The shadows of the Doji would be seen as gapped below the lower shadow of the first candle.

The third candle would be a white candle. The closing of the third candle would be well into the body of the first candle.

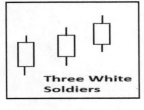

#8 Three White Soldiers: Three White Soldier Pattern indicates a strong reversal signal. This pattern consists of three candles. All the three candles would be a white candle that would be either of a normal size or long. The three candles would move upwards.

The open price of each candle would be lower than the previous candle's close price. But each candle's prices would close at higher levels.

Bearish Candlestick Patterns

The candlestick patterns that indicate a bearish bias for the market is called as Bearish candlestick patterns.

These patterns can be used for identifying good exit points for a trade, as well as for setting stop loss levels.

Following are some of the important bearish candlestick patterns:

- Bearish Engulfing

- Bearish Dark Cloud Cover

- Bearish Shooting star

- Hanging Man

- Bearish Belt Hold

- Bearish Harami/ Harami Cross

- Bearish Doji Star

- Bearish Abandoned Baby

- Bearish Evening Star

#1 Bearish Engulfing: Bearish Engulfing pattern indicates an upcoming top reversal and happens during an uptrend. It comprises of two candlesticks. The first candle would be a small white candle.

The second candle would be a long black candle which would completely engulf the body (but not necessarily the shadows) of the first day's white candle.

#2 Bearish Dark Cloud cover: Bearish Dark Cloud Cover is a top

290

reversal pattern that takes place during a bull run. This pattern consists of two candlesticks. The first candle would be a white one.

The second candle would be a black candle which opens at a new high with a gap up and closes more than halfway into the body of first day's candle.

#3 Bearish Shooting star: Bearish Shooting 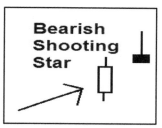 star pattern indicates an upcoming trend reversal of the prevailing bull market. This pattern consists of two candlesticks. The first candle would be a white candle.

The second candle would be an inverted hammer with a small body and a long shadow at the top.

#4 Bearish Belt Hold: Bearish Belt Hold  pattern is formed during a price uptrend and indicates an upcoming reversal of trend to bear market. This pattern consists of a single black candlestick. The candle would open at a high price for the day and would close at the low price of the day (or very near to it), resulting in a tall black candle.

#5 Bearish Harami/ Harami Cross:

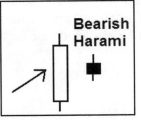

Bearish Harami, as well as Harami Cross, are bearish reversal patterns that comprise of two candlesticks.

In Bearish Harami Pattern, the first candle would be a tall white candle.

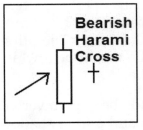

The second candle would be a black candle that would have a small body. This second candle would be completely within the range of the first candlestick's body.

In the case of Bearish Harami Cross pattern, there is just one minor difference – the second candlestick would be a doji.

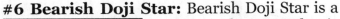

#6 Bearish Doji Star: Bearish Doji Star is a

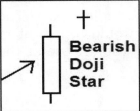

top reversal pattern that is seen during a bullish uptrend. It consists of two candles. The first candle

292

would be a long white candle. The second candle would open with an upward gap and its body would remain higher than that of the first candle's body. The second candle would close with the price almost the same as open price, resulting in a doji. The length of the shadow of the second candle would also be short.

#7 Bearish Abandoned Baby: Bearish Abandoned Baby is a rare bearish reversal candlestick pattern. It consists of three candles. The first candle would be a white candle.

The second candle would be a doji that would be formed by gapping upwards. The shadow of this doji would remain above the high of the first candle.

The third candle would be a black candle which would be formed gapped down below the second candle. The upper shadow of this third black candle would be below the low of the second (doji) candle.

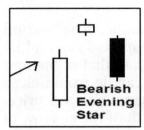

#8 Bearish Evening Star: Bearish Evening Star candlestick pattern foretells an upcoming bearish reversal. It consists of three candlesticks.

The first candle would be a long white candle formed during a price uptrend.

The second candle would be a small white/black candle that gaps up above the body of the first candle.

The third candle would be a tall black candle. The open price of this third candle would be below the second candle. The close price of the third candle would be at least mid-way of the body of the first candle.

Although there are few more candlestick patterns in existence, the above-mentioned candlesticks are the most vital ones.

Important Technical indicators for Penny Stocks

Before moving onto the advanced strategies for Buying as well as Exiting Penny Stocks, you must have a good understanding of the some of the important technical indicators of Penny Stocks. Here, you will be given a brief overview of the following– RSI, MACD, Stochastic, and Bollinger Bands.

RSI

RSI or Relative Strength Index indicates the momentum of a stock. This bound oscillator (of range 0 to 100) is used for identifying overbought and oversold levels of the security.

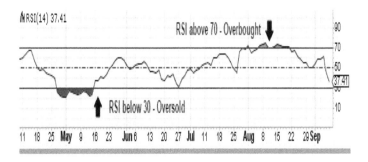

(Fig) RSI indicator

- When the value of RSI is **above** 70, it is considered as **overbought**.

- When the value of RSI is **below** 30, it is considered as **oversold.**

Full Stochastic Oscillator

Full Stochastic Oscillator, typically called as stochastics is a momentum indicator. It is used for identifying overbought and oversold levels of a security.

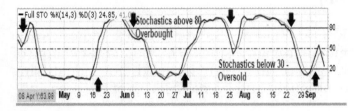

(Fig) Full Stochastic Oscillator

- When the value of Stochastics is **above** 80, it is considered as **overbought**.

- When the value of Stochastics is **below** 20, it is considered as **oversold.**

MACD

MACD or Moving Average Convergence Divergence is a simple as well as efficient momentum indicator that can be used for trend following as well. MACD consists of three parts – MACD line, Signal Line, and MACD Histogram.

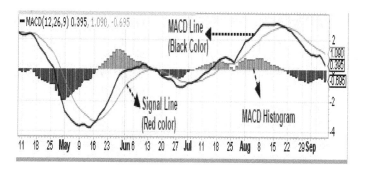

(Fig) MACD Indicator

MACD Line is typically a black line. It is formed when the 12 day EMA of the closing price of security is subtracted from 26-day EMA of the closing price of the security. In short,

- MACD Line = (26-day EMA − 12 day EMA) of stock's closing price

Signal Line is typically red in color. It is the 9 day EMA of MACD Line. In short,

- Signal Line = 9-day EMA of MACD Line

MACD Histogram is formed by decreasing Signal Line from MACD Line

- MACD Histogram = MACD Signal Line – MACD Line

- MACD Histogram is **positive** when MACD Line crosses above Signal Line

- MACD Histogram is **negative** when MACD Line crosses below Signal Line

Bollinger Bands

Bollinger bands are volatility indicators. It comprises of an upper band, lower band, and middle band.

- Middle band is the 20 day SMA

The upper band is found by adding 20-day SMA with a 20-day standard deviation of price multiplied by 2.

- Upper band = 20 day SMA + (2 X 20 day standard deviation of price)

The lower band is found by subtracting the 20-day standard deviation of price multiplied by 2 from 20-day SMA.

- Lower band = 20-day SMA - (2 X 20-day standard deviation of price)

298

(Fig) Bollinger Bands

- If the price moves towards the top of Bollinger band, the prices are said to be high

- If the price moves towards the bottom of Bollinger band, the prices are said to be low

CHAPTER 3: PENNY STOCKS –

ADVANCED ANALYSIS

Importance of Tools and Resources for picking out Penny Stock winners

Out of the numerous Penny Stock available, identifying good ones by trial and error is simply not feasible. Not only is it time-consuming, it is also a highly exhausting and mind-numbing process.

This is where the mentality of a smart investor is different. He or she would make use of available tools and resources (like stock screeners) for picking out Penny Stocks that fits specific criteria.

Before we get into the details pertaining to Stock Screeners, below are the important tips for picking out companies that are Penny Stock winners and the red flags to look out for in order to identify the Penny Stock losers.

How to identify potential Penny Stock Winners?

A quick and easy way to identify a potential winner amongst Penny Stocks is to watch out for the following characteristics of the company:

#1 *Valuation:* In case the company has a low market cap when compared to its sales or book value, it indicates that the company has a good valuation. The stocks of such company have a high probability of breaking out and giving lots of profit to the investor.

#2 *High Growth Rate:* Verify if the company is reporting high growth quarter on quarter. Even if the year on year growth doesn't seem exceptional, the company is a potential multi-bagger in case its quarter-to-quarter growth for previous two to three quarters are phenomenal.

#3 *Cash reserves:* Check out the cash reserves of the company before investing in its stocks. The rule of thumb is that companies with good cash reserves are highly likely to provide good returns.

How to avoid Penny Stock Losers – Major Red flags to look for

Below are some of the red flags to look out for in order to identify Penny Stock Losers. Avoid trading the stock of such companies as far as possible

#1 *Cash balance lower than $250,000:* When looking at the asset column of the company's balance sheet, if the cash balance is less than $250,000, it is best to avoid such companies.

#2 *Long term and Short term Debt:* Avoid the Penny Stocks that has a

- Short Term Debt higher than Cash balance.

- Long-term Debt higher than Zero.

#3 *Signs of Pump and Dump scheme:* It is best to be cautious about stocks that get aggressively promoted using press releases, insider information, newsletters, bulletin boards etc. Such actions indicate a probable pumping activity done by pump and dump schemes.

How to take advantage of Stock Screeners

There are numerous stock screeners available that can be used for picking out Penny Stock winners. Some of them are paid – like OptionsXpress while some others are free –

like busystock or OTC market stock screeners. The functionalities available for these stock screeners also varies depending on the cost. Below is a guideline for using these stock screeners effectively.

- Pick a price range for the stock you intend to trade or invest in. Then set the price filter to that range (say, under $1).

- Adjust the volume filter to a higher setting in order to select stocks with high volume levels. Doing so will help you find stocks that have a good liquidity.

- If interested, include any technical or fundamental analysis indicators as well in the filter criteria. This is optional.

- Click on the search button to get a list of Penny Stocks that fulfill all your selected search criteria.

- Among the resulting list of stocks, check for any alerts regarding scams, bankruptcy, or fraud. Eliminate those stocks from the list.

- From the resultant list, apply the appropriate trading strategies (mentioned in the next chapter) in order to find the entry as well as exit criteria for the stock.

Thus, stock screeners can be effectively used for eliminating undesirable stocks while refining the search criteria for picking out Penny Stock winners.

Chapter 4: Advanced Strategies for Buying a Penny Stock

Various buying strategies can be used for Penny Stocks depending upon the prevailing trend of the stock.

Case 1: Advanced strategies for Stocks in Uptrend

This section contains advanced strategies for identifying the buy level for Penny Stocks that are in an uptrend. In case of a Penny Stock that in a strong uptrend, following two strategies can be used to take a long position at appropriate times

- Advanced buying strategy using moving averages cross over and Stochastics

- Advanced strategy using multi-time frames and RSI

#1: Advanced buying strategy using moving averages cross over and Stochastics

Advanced buying strategy using moving averages cross over and Stochastics is based on the combination of two moving averages and the stochastics on the weekly chart of the Penny Stock. The basic concept is to buy the

Penny Stock on the breakout after a long period of consolidation.

Trading Strategy: The trading strategy involves the crossover of two moving averages. Among the two moving averages, one should be of shorter duration and the other of a longer duration. The two moving averages that are best suited for this strategy are the 20-week moving average and the 50-week moving average. These two moving averages would then be used in conjunction with the stochastic indicator to get the entry signal.

Most Penny Stocks consolidate for a long period of time before breaking out of a range and starting the uptrend. The moving averages help in entering the stock when the momentum starts building up.

Identifying Uptrend: Once the price starts to trade above the moving averages and the shorter moving average crosses above the longer moving average, the stock is said to be in an uptrend.

Entry Criteria: The entry signal for the strategy is as follows

- The price starts to trade above both the moving averages.

- The shorter moving average crosses above the longer moving average.

- Stochastic is in the oversold region.

This is best explained using an example.

Example: Following is the chart of a Penny Stock Independence Energy Stock (IDNG). According to the strategy, the entry signal for going long on this Penny Stock would be when

- IDNG starts trading above the two moving averages

- The 20 day WMA crosses the 50 WMA.

- Stochastic is oversold.

The entry signal is marked on the chart below.

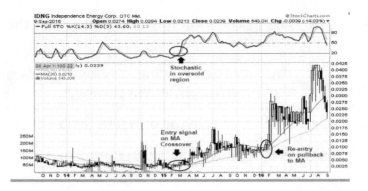

     (Fig) Strategy using Moving Averages cross over and Stochastics

Re-entry during Correction: For traders who missed out on buying the stock on the initial buy signal, they can look to enter the stock on corrections. Such re-entry points are also marked on the chart.

Ideally, the re-entry should be when the stock corrects to the space between the two moving averages. A bullish reversal candle forming in the space between the moving averages is an ideal point to enter the stock after a correction.

#2: Advanced buying strategy using multi-time frames and RSI.

Advanced buying strategy using multi-time frames and RSI involves analyzing the stock on the daily and the weekly time frame and checking if the RSI levels indicate a favorable entry setup. Analyzing the stock using both daily as well as weekly time frames would provide an added margin of safety and help in fine tuning the entry.

Trading Strategy: First, the stock would be analyzed on the weekly chart. It should fulfill a specific set of criteria on the weekly chart. Then, the stock would be analyzed on the daily charts. Once it fulfills a specific set of conditions on the daily chart as well, entry can be made for the stock as long as the RSI is in the specific range of values.

Entry Criteria – Analyzing Weekly Chart: Following are the conditions to be fulfilled on the weekly chart.

- The stock should be in an **uptrend** on the weekly chart. This means that the stock should make higher highs and higher lows on the weekly chart.

- The stock should be trading above the **30-day** moving average.

- The **RSI** should be either

- In the oversold region – ie, 20 or below

- Above 20 and moving in an upwards direction; but not yet reached the overbought region (i.e. above 80)
- High volume **bearish reversal candles** (hanging man, doji, evening star etc.) should **not** be formed on the weekly chart.

Once the above criteria are met on the weekly charts, the stock should then be analyzed on the daily chart to get an entry point.

Entry Criteria – Analyzing Daily Chart: Once the weekly uptrend is established, following conditions in the daily chart can be used for taking a long position

- The stock corrects and takes **support** at the **trend line**. Ideally, the stock should form a bullish reversal candle (hammer, morning star etc.) near the trend line.

- The **RSI** should be either

- In the oversold region i.e. 20 or below
- Above 20 and moving in an upwards direction; but not yet reached the overbought region (i.e. above 80)

The basic premise is to buy on pullbacks or corrections on the daily chart while the main trend on the weekly chart remains intact.

This strategy is best explained with an example.

Example: Following is the chart of a Penny Stock Kraig Biocraft Laboratories Inc (KBLB). According to the strategy, an entry signal is generated in the weekly chart for going long on this Penny Stock due to the following reasons.

- On the weekly chart of KBLB, the stock has been making higher highs and higher lows indicating that the stock is in an uptrend.

- The RSI is 60 which is below the overbought area, so there is more room for the uptrend to continue.

- KBLB is trading above 30-day SMA.

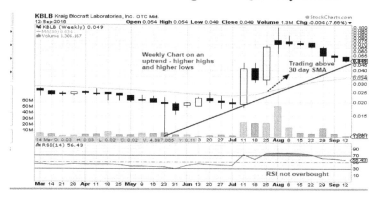

(Fig) Entry on weekly charts: Multi-time frames and RSI strategy

Next, we need to move on to the daily chart of KBLB to get a suitable entry point.

As per the daily chart of KBLB, an entry signal is generated for the stock due to the following reasons.

- The stock has corrected back to the trend line.

- A bullish reversal candle (hammer), has formed in this area which means that the immediate downtrend is over and the stock has taken support in this region.

- The RSI is above 20 and moving up.

(Fig) Entry on daily charts: Multi-time frames and RSI strategy

So the conditions are satisfied on the daily chart as well and hence, the buy signal is generated. This is marked on the chart.

The past buy signal is also marked on the chart.

Case 2: Advanced strategies for stocks that breakout from a range

The next two strategies can be used when a Penny Stock breaks out of a range. Most Penny Stock consolidates for a long time before making a big up move. The period of consolidation can last from a few weeks to a few months. It is important to make an entry only after the breakout is validated to avoid false breakouts.

Following are the strategies for trading stocks that breakout from a range:

- Advanced buying strategy using Bollinger bands and MACD lines

- Advanced buying strategy using price action and volume

#3: Advanced buying strategy using Bollinger bands and MACD lines

Advanced buying strategy using Bollinger bands and MACD lines makes use of MACD lines as well as Bollinger Bands to determine the entry point of the trade. This strategy is highly useful for buying Penny Stock just before they break out of a narrow range.

Settings: The settings of Bollinger bands and MACD to be used for this strategy is their default settings.

Trading Strategy: First, scan for stocks that have a Bollinger squeeze. The scan is done either manually by checking each stock individually or by making use of the scan feature that some trading platforms provide.

Note: Bollinger squeeze is said to occur when the volatility is low and the Bollinger band narrows.

In most cases, a big move follows after a period of low volatility. So, after identifying the stock that has a Bollinger squeeze, you must wait for the stock to breakout of the squeeze or in other words, wait for the Bollinger band to expand.

Entry Criteria: The buy signal is generated when the following conditions are satisfied.

- When the stock breaks out of the squeeze

- When the fast moving MACD line crosses the slow moving line.

This is best explained with the help of an example.

Example: Following is the chart of a Penny Stock Amarin Corp PLC ADS (AMRN). As you can see from the chart, the stock was in a Bollinger squeeze initially. This period of Bollinger Squeeze is marked on the chart.

This Bollinger Squeeze indicates a period of low volatility. During this period of low volatility, the stock should be kept on the radar, but no action should be taken.

Following is the entry criteria for the trade.

- Once the stock breaks out of the squeeze and the band expands a buy signal is generated. This is marked on the chart below.

- In order to confirm the strength of the breakout, the MACD lines should crossover as well.

Once these two criteria are met, an entry can be made into the stock. As seen from the chart, a big up move followed the period of low volatility or the Bollinger squeeze.

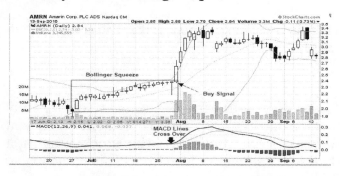

(Fig) Strategy using Bollinger Bands and MACD Lines

In a nutshell, this strategy can be summarized as

- Scan for stocks that have Bollinger squeeze and keep them on the watch list

- Wait for the stock to break out of the squeeze and for the band to expand.

- Take a long position when the MACD lines crossover.

#4: Advanced buying strategy using price action and volume

Advanced buying strategy using price action and volume is based on the price action and the corresponding volume of a Penny Stock. As mentioned earlier, most Penny Stocks undergo a period of consolidation before a breakout or an uptrend. But first, it is important to understand a few basic concepts regarding price action before we delve deeper into this strategy.

A prerequisite for understanding this strategy would be a basic comprehension about candlesticks. A long (wide), green (white) candle usually indicates that a strong up move has happened. But it is important to use this in conjunction with volume to get a bigger picture.

- A long candle with high volume indicates that the up move is backed

317

by strong hands or smart money, whereas

- A long candle with low volume might not necessarily indicate that the buying was by smart money.

Note: The term **smart money** refers to strong financial institutions like banks, mutual funds etc., or foreign investors. It is important to remain on the same side as the smart money to raises your odds of a profitable trade. So, identifying the price action is very important.

Similarly, a narrow green (white) candle with a high volume might not be a good sign because it indicates that the smart money was distributing or selling the stock.

Trading strategy: According to this strategy, first identify Penny Stocks that are consolidating or in a range. In most cases, the Penny Stocks would be consolidating inside a channel. Then go for long positions when breakout happens supported with huge volume surge.

Entry Criteria: The entry signal for this strategy would be triggered when the stock breaks out the channel or range on high volumes. The term high volumes imply volumes that are at least 5 times the normal volume levels of the previous 6 months.

This is best explained with an example.

Example: Following is the chart of a Penny Stock Northern Dynasty Minerals Limited (NDK). As you can see from the chart, NAK was consolidating inside a channel for several weeks before it finally broke out of the channel.

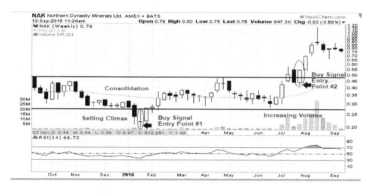

  (Fig) Strategy using Price action and Volume

Following are the two entry points for taking long positions.

- At the lower end of the channel whenever there is a long legged

319

candle. This usually indicates a selling climax before a big up move begins. Selling climax is nothing but the shaking out of weaker hands by the smart money. This is the entry point # 1 marked on the chart

- When the price breaks out of the channel on high volumes. This is marked as entry point # 2 on the chart.

The second entry point is safer because the entry is made only after the breakout occurs from the range. But on the downside, it would be less profitable than the trades done at entry point # 1.

Case 3: Advanced strategy for Pre- Spike Identification

This section is probably the most anticipated one. Here, you will be learning about trading strategies that can be used to identify Penny Stock winners pre-spike. After all, the early bird gets the worm et all.

Following are the advanced strategies:

- Advanced buying strategy using MACD histogram positive divergence

- Advanced buying strategy using bullish candlestick patterns

#5: Advanced buying strategy using MACD histogram positive divergence

Advanced buying strategy using MACD histogram positive divergence is useful for buying beaten down Penny Stocks. This strategy helps in identifying stocks which have a positive divergence in MACD histogram and price. Such divergence indicates that the down momentum of the stock is weakening and a reversal is around the corner.

A prerequisite for understanding this strategy would be a basic comprehension about MACD histogram and divergence.

MACD Histogram: Like mentioned earlier, MACD Histogram is the difference between the fast moving MACD line and the signal line. This difference is then plotted to get a histogram. The MACD histogram is very useful in finding divergences.

Divergence: Although there are several different types of divergences, the divergence referenced here is the price and the MACD divergence.

So what exactly is a divergence? A positive divergence occurs when

- The price makes a lower low but

- The indicator (MACD histogram in this case), makes a higher low.

Trading Strategy: First, identify the stocks that are currently at a beaten down level, but shows a positive divergence between MACD Histogram and price. Such a positive divergence indicates that even though the price was driven lower to make a lower low, the indicator did not follow suit. This essentially means that the downward momentum is reducing and a possible reversal is around the corner for the stock.

Entry Criteria: The entry should be made as soon as the MACD histogram starts moving up. This means that the entry point would be the next candle after the upmove starts for MACD Histogram.

This is best explained with an example.

Example: Following is the chart of a Penny Stock Amarin Corp PLC ADS (AMRN). This can be used to understand the price and MACD divergence as well as when an entry signal is generated.

The stock of was on a down trend making lower lows and lower highs. In the month of February, the stock made a lower low, but the MACD histogram made a higher low. This indicated that the selling pressure was reducing and the stock was on the brink of a possible reversal.

The buy signal for this setup would be when the MACD histogram makes a shorter bar or starts moving up. This is marked on the chart below. As can be seen from the chart, the stock rallied from there on after.

(Fig) Strategy using MACD Histogram - Price positive divergence

This method is quite useful in identifying beaten down Penny Stocks but it's important to understand that there is no guarantee that this method would work all the time. After all technical analysis just raises our odds of success. So it is important to keep a Stop loss. The ideal stop loss would be a few cents below the last pivot low.

#6: Advanced buying strategy using bullish candlestick patterns

Bullish candlestick patterns indicate that the demand is greater than the supply. When the demand is greater than the supply, only longs should be taken. There are several bullish candlestick patterns, and some of the important ones have been discussed earlier in the book.

Trading Strategy: First, identify the stocks which have bullish candlestick patterns being formed. Then use these bullish candlestick patterns in conjunction with an indicator like RSI or Stochastic to get a more accurate buy signal.

In order to get a more accurate and reliable buy signal, it is better to use the weekly chart while using this strategy.

Let us understand this strategy using two bullish candlestick patterns: the hammer and the bullish inside bar (Bullish Harami).

Hammer: The hammer is usually formed at the end of a downtrend. Since it has a long wick, it indicates that even though the stock went down over the week, there was buying pressure causing the stock to bounce back towards the end of the week. This is a strong bullish candlestick.

Bullish Harami: The bullish inside bar (or Bullish Harami) is usually formed after a big black (bearish) candle i.e. after a week where the stock moved down drastically.

The candle formed after the black candle is called an inside bar if its entire range remains within the range of the previous candle. Some people also call it an inside bar even if just the body of the candle remains within the range of the previous week's candle.

The candle referred here is a weekly candle, as the strategy involves the use of a weekly time frame. (Inside bar can form in any time frame.)

Entry Criteria - Hammer: The entry can be made when

- The Hammer pattern is formed on the weekly chart, and

- RSI is in the oversold region.

- RSI can also be slightly above the oversold region and moving up

This is best explained with an example.

Example: In the below chart of FTR, the stock was in a downtrend making lower highs and lower lows. On the week of Jan 2016, the stock made a hammer pattern.

This indicated that the demand was increasing, probably because the buyers felt that the stock was now trading at a fair value. At the same time, RSI was in the oversold region, further confirming the buy signal.

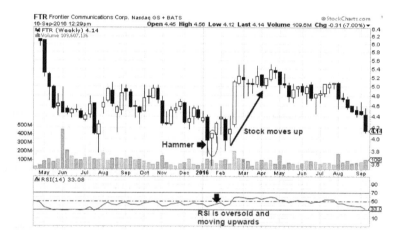

(Fig) Hammer and RSI

The stop loss for the trade would be a few pips below the low of the hammer. As we can see from the chart, the stock rallied from there on in.

Entry Criteria – Bullish Harami: The entry can be made when

- The Inside Bar pattern is formed on the weekly chart, and

- RSI is in the oversold region.

- RSI can also be slightly above the oversold region and moving up

This is best explained with an example.

Example: In the chart of MNKD the stock has been on a downtrend. On the week of January 2016, the stock formed a big black candle. In the week that followed, the stock formed an inside bar as can be seen from the chart.

This indicated that the selling pressure has reduced. The buyers were now back, probably because they felt that the stock has reached a region of fair value now.

The RSI was also in the oversold region, thus generating a buy signal.

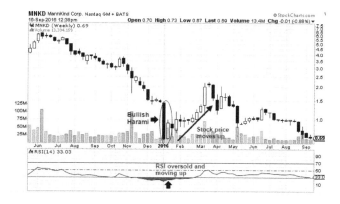

(Fig) Bullish Harami and RSI

Alternate Trading Strategy using Bullish Candlestick Patterns:

Another strategy to use the bullish candlesticks for an entry point is to wait for a bullish reversal candlestick in important *support areas*. Once the bullish candle is formed in the support area, it validates the strength of the support area. These areas are good *entry points*.

This again can be used in conjunction with RSI to identify an even better entry point. Ideally,

- The RSI should be in the oversold region.

- RSI can also be slightly above the oversold region and moving up.

CHAPTER 5: ADVANCED STRATEGIES FOR EXITING A PENNY STOCK

Exiting a trade is equally important as entering a trade. There are mainly three reasons for it.

- The profits become real only once the trade is completed.

- Exiting at the correct point will prevent losing all the profits made till then.

- In order to short sell a Penny Stock, although this is not advised.

Hence, it is vital that you understand the selling strategies for exiting Penny Stocks. It is important to book profits on the first sign of weakness especially in Penny Stocks.

What is an Exit strategy? Exit strategies are basically combinations of patterns and indicators that help in identifying the possible tops from where the market could correct drastically.

Essentially, exit strategies help in identifying weakness or selling pressure, right when it starts.

Following are some important selling strategies for Penny Stocks that would help in exiting from a Penny Stock before it starts going down.

- Advanced Exit Strategy based on negative MACD divergence

- Advanced Exit Strategy based on Moving Averages crossover

- Advanced Exit Strategy based on Trendline Breakdown

- Advanced Exit Strategy based on RSI negative divergence

- Advanced Exit Strategy based on bearish candlestick patterns

#1 Advanced Exit Strategy based on negative MACD divergence

A Divergence occurs when the price and the indicator start behaving differently. A negative divergence occurs when the price makes higher highs but the indicator makes lower highs. This basically indicates that even the stock has been moving higher, the momentum has been weakening. This indicates that a possible bearish reversal is around the corner.

Trading Strategy: First, check for any negative divergence between MACD and Price. In case there is an MACD negative divergence,

- The price would make a higher high but

- Either the MACD lines or MACD histogram makes a lower high.

Exit Criteria: The exit should be made as soon as the MACD histogram starts moving down. This means that the exit point would be

- The next candle after the down move starts for MACD Histogram Or,

- MACD forms a shorter histogram bar

This is best explained with an example.

Example: In the chart of NETE, the price has been moving up as shown in the chart. But this move was not supported by the MACD as it was making lower highs.

So once this setup has been identified, the exit signal would be on the candlestick where the MACD forms a shorter histogram bar. These have been marked on the chart.

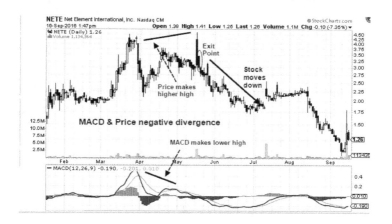

(Fig) MACD – Price negative divergence Exit Strategy

As seen from the chart, the stock corrected drastically after that.

#2 Advanced Exit Strategy based on RSI negative divergence

333

This strategy is similar to the MACD divergence. The only difference is that RSI is used instead of MACD.

The divergence occurs when the price makes a higher high and the RSI makes a lower high, indicating that the momentum is reducing.

Example: In the chart of NETE, the price made a higher high in April – May 2016, but the RSI made a lower high at the same time.

Once the pattern is identified, the exit signal is triggered when the stock forms a bearish reversal candle. All these have been marked on the chart below.

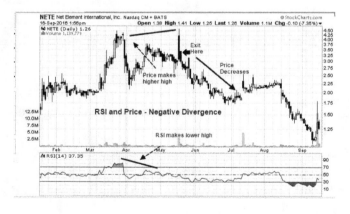

(Fig) RSI – Price negative divergence Exit Strategy

#3 Advanced Exit Strategy based on Moving Averages crossover

Moving averages can be used to determine if the stock is losing momentum. In case the stock starts to lose momentum, exiting the stock can be considered.

Typically, the 200-day moving average is used to decide the trend of a stock. It is considered bullish if the stock is trading above the 200-day moving average and bearish if it is trading below it.

There are two trading strategies based on how risk averse you are with respect to trading Penny Stocks.

Trading Strategy 1: After an uptrend, if the stock corrects and closes below the 200-day moving average, then it indicates that the uptrend is over and exiting the stock right then would be a good option.

Trading Strategy 2: However, if the stock were to close below the 200-day moving average, it would have already corrected to a good extent. Hence, your exit would become a tad late. For traders who want to make a faster exit, pick the exit signal based on the combination of 20-day and 50-day moving average.

Exit Criteria for Trading Strategy 2:
The exit signal is triggered when

- The price closes below the 20-day moving average
- The 20-day moving average crosses below the 50-day moving average

This indicates a short-term weakness and an exit can be planned.

This is best explained using an example.

Example: The stock COSI was in a steady uptrend making higher highs and higher lows. On last week of April, the stock closed below its 20-day moving average and soon after the 20-day moving average crossed below the 50-day moving average, generating an exit signal.

(Fig) Exit Strategy using moving averages crossover

As can be seen from the chart, the stock corrected substantially after that.

Any combination of moving averages can be used for this strategy. It is important to back test and see which combination works well in a particular market for a particular stock. A few of the other common combinations are 10 and 30, 15 and 40 and 50 and 200.

#4 Advanced Exit Strategy based on Trendline Breakdown

When a stock is in an uptrend, it usually makes a series of well-defined higher lows or pivot lows.

337

A pivot low is the last low made before the stock makes a new high. These pivot lows or higher lows can be joined to form a *trend line*.

In most cases as long as the trend is up, the stock respects the trend line. In other words, when the stock corrects and reaches the trend line, it is considered to be of fair value and demand exists. Thus, the stock takes support at the trend line. So as long as the stock holds this trend line it can be said to be in an uptrend.

Trading Strategy: First, identify the stocks in an uptrend with a clear defined trend line. Once the stock goes below the trend line, it shows that the trend is weakening. Make the exit when the exit signal is triggered.

Exit Criteria: Following are the conditions for the exit.

- When the stock goes below trend line

- If the stock goes below the previous pivot low.

This would indicate that the uptrend has indeed ended.

This is best explained with an example.

Example: In the chart of FTR, the stock was in a strong uptrend making higher highs and higher lows. A trend line has been drawn on the chart by joining all the pivot lows.

In the month of June 2015, the stock broke down from the trend line. Traders who are risk averse can even consider exiting the stock at this point (Exit #1).

But it is better to wait for the stock to go below the previous pivot low (Exit #2) to make sure that the trend has indeed ended.

(Fig) Exit Strategy based on trend line breakdown

As seen from the chart, a few days later, the stock goes below the previous pivot low, indicating that the trend is over.

It is better to exit the stock at this point as a period of the uptrend is usually followed either by sideways movement or a down trend.

#5 Advanced Exit Strategy based on bearish candlestick patterns

Candlesticks patterns give a good indication of the balance between supply and demand. Bullish candlestick patterns are those which indicate that the demand is greater than the supply. Conversely, bearish reversal candles indicate that the supply is greater than the demand. For now, only in the bearish reversal candles would be discussed as the focus is on exit strategies.

Trading Strategy: First, identify the stocks which have ***bearish*** candlestick patterns being formed. Note that candlesticks should not be used as a standalone tool for exiting a stock. Hence, these bearish candlestick patterns should be used in conjunction with an indicator like ***stochastics***.

It is better to use these candlestick patterns on the weekly chart for determining the exit point from a Penny Stock. Various bearish candlestick patterns have been discussed earlier in this book. Here, the focus is given a bearish pattern – bearish engulfing with relevant examples.

Exit Criteria – Bearish Engulfing: The exit can be made when

- The Bearish Engulfing pattern is formed on the weekly chart, and

- Stochastic is in the overbought region.

- RSI can also be slightly above the overbought region and moving down

This is best explained with an example.

Example: In the chart below of GERN the stock was on an uptrend, making higher highs and higher lows. The stock formed a bearish engulfing with good volumes in December 2015.

Bearish engulfing is a major reversal candle and it indicates that the supply is getting stronger. The bearish engulfing candle completely covered the range of the previous candle, indicating strong supply.

(Fig) Bearish Engulfing and Stochastic

At the same time, Stochastic was in the overbought zone. This further confirms the weakness and an exit signal is generated. The stock went down after the exit signal was generated.

CHAPTER 6: MONEY

MANAGEMENT

Successful investing as well as trading in Penny Stocks require clear and defined money management rules and tips. They help in reigning in the losses while maximizing the profits. This chapter on money management deals precisely with this concept. For ease of understanding, it is divided into two sections

- Money management for Penny Stocks trading
- Money management for Penny Stocks investment

Money management for Penny Stocks trading

Trading can yield both profits as well as losses. But many times, traders are unsure about when to book the profits. They keep on holding the stock in anticipation that the trade would turn more profitable, and may eventually have to sell at a loss.

Conversely, many traders hold onto losing trades in the anticipation and hope that the tide will turn and the trade would become profitable. This could result in massive losses.

The following section contains guidelines and tips on when to book profits as well as when to take losses. These tips can be used in conjunction with the various exit strategies mentioned in the earlier chapter.

#1 When to book profits?

For trades which are at a profit, the ideal position to exit is in the following cases

- When the price of the stock is significantly higher than the original buy price, look into booking at least half of the purchased quantity. This strategy also makes the holding of the remaining stocks less risky.

- In case there is any breaking news that seems unfavorable to the company whose stocks that you are holding, exit the stock immediately and book profits.

- When the stocks start trading at a high price, but with a low volume, it shows signs of weakening of stock. Hence, it is best to book profits and exit the trade.

#2 When to take losses?

Following are tips to exit trades which are at a loss

- When the stop loss level is reached – Many times, traders hold onto stock even when it reaches the stock's planned stop loss, leading to additional losses. It is always best to simply exit the trade at planned stop loss. This helps in maintaining the trading discipline as well.

- In case the trade was taken based on the rumors pertaining to specific upcoming developments of the company, check the price action after the said event comes to fruition. If the stock price is not moving well despite the development, it is best to ditch the stock even at a loss.

- If there is a huge increase in the trading volume without much changes happening in the price, it is a **bad** sign. It signifies a potential sell-off from investors. Hence, it is best to exit the trade when such a phenomenon is observed, even if you have to book losses.

Money management for Penny Stocks investment

Unlike trading, investment requires long-term planning. Following are two important strategies for Penny Stock investment:

- Position Sizing
- Dollar cost averaging

Importance of Dollar Cost Averaging

One of the most common mistakes done by both novice Penny Stock investors and veterans alike is to buy the entire quantity of stocks (that is intended to be purchased) on a single day itself. The stock market is too fluid, as its direction changes based on even a rumor or breaking news. Due to this, you would not be able to plan the exact moment to invest in a stock in such a manner that it would maximize your profit.

This is best explained with an example. Assume that you invested in 2000 stocks of company XYZ on Monday costing you $2000 in total.

Case1: On Tuesday, the CEO of the company resigns due to some accounting scandal. The market reacts to the news and the stock corrects from $1 to $0.65. Had you waited for a day before making the investment, you could have bought 2000 stocks of the company for $1300, effectively saving you $700.

Case 2: Conversely, assume that a product of the company XYZ won a patent on Tuesday, causing its stock price to rise to $1.30 from the original $1. Had you waited for another day to invest, you would have had to shell out $2600, which is $600 more than the previous day!

As you can see, it is difficult to precisely time when the investment should be made. Depending on the news of the day, the price of the stock could either increase or decrease. This is where the Dollar Cost Averaging (or Pound Cost Averaging) strategy gains importance.

What is Dollar Cost Averaging? In Dollar cost averaging strategy, the stock is bought using a fixed sum of money on a specific schedule (say, every 3 months or 6 months) regardless of the stock's price. Typically, the number of stocks purchased are low when the stock price is high, while a higher number of stocks are bought when the stock price is lower.

Why Dollar Cost Averaging?

- By using this strategy, the average price of the stock would be lower in comparison to the bulk purchase.

- It also lowers the probability of risking a huge amount at a wrong time.

- The recommended wait period between two purchases is six months to a year.

- Although it might result in a higher broker commission, the overall benefit surpasses the higher broker cost.

Uses of Dollar Cost Averaging: Dollar Cost Averaging strategy is highly useful in protecting your investment against

- The market's downside risk as well as

- Market fluctuations.

Risk: This strategy does not protect the money in case the stock you had invested in is in a free fall. This can be avoided to an extent by researching the stock thoroughly (including the technical as well as fundamental analysis) before doing the investment.

Who should use this strategy? This strategy is ideal for Penny Stock investors who are

- Risk averse

- Looking for long term investment

- Wants to invest in a stock which is historically volatile in its price.

- Looking into investing in a market which is in a temporary downtrend.

Importance of Position sizing

Another important strategy pertaining to Penny Stock investing is Position Sizing. This is one of the most misunderstood, albeit powerful investing strategy. It is based on purely mathematical calculations and help in controlling risks while providing maximum profits.

What is position sizing? The concept of position sizing is to basically set a percentage limit or dollar limit of the individual's portfolio for purchasing stocks. This is best explained using hypothetical portfolio and stock example.

Assume that an individual's total portfolio is worth $100,000

- If $5000 worth of stock 'ABC' is present in the portfolio, it means that ABC has a position size of 5%.

- On the other hand, if $15,000 worth of stock 'LMN' is present in the portfolio, it has a position size of 15%.

The basic idea of position sizing strategy is to *limit* the percentage of your account in a single position. For instance, you can set the *limit as 4%*.

In that case, in the $100,000 portfolio, no stock should be present which is worth more than 4% of the total value (or $4000).

Why position sizing?

- Prevents catastrophic losses to the portfolio

- Diversifies portfolio

- Safeguards portfolio against market crashes to an extent

Risk: This downside of this strategy is that it limits the profits. For example, assume that the stock 'PQR' of your portfolio had a huge move upwards. (say, from $1 to $2) Had you invested in this stock for say, around 90% of the portfolio, your portfolio would have gained huge profits. But since the percentage value of the stock in the portfolio is limited to just 5%, the profits gained are also limited.

Who should use this strategy? This strategy is ideal for Penny Stock investors

- Who have a large portfolio

- Who wants to avoid substantial losses to their portfolio

Note: The concept of position sizing can also be used in case of Penny Stock Trading. The rule of thumb here is that more than 1% of the trading capital should not be risked in a single trade. For example, if your trading account is for $500, you should not risk more than $5 on a trade.

Bonus Chapter: Secrets for

Successful Penny Stock

Trading

In order to become a successful Penny Stock Trader, you would need experience as well as education in equal measures. Educating yourself is an easier process, as you can simply read books or attend seminars. Experience, however, is a tricky thing, as it is not always written about in stock trading books.

In this bonus section, I will be disclosing some of my rules for trading Penny Stocks that has helped me maximize profits over the years.

1. Always have an exit plan in mind. Cut the losses and exit from trades if the trade doesn't go as planned. Remember that your wins from successful trades would quickly cover these small losses.

2. Keep a diary of your successful and not-so-successful trades. This will help you find out which trading style suits you the best, giving you maximum profits. Eventually, a trading framework can be built, and can be fine-tuned every now and then.

3. Avoid Penny Stocks that have a very low liquidity. Chances are, you will be stuck with those and unable to exit them as there are no buyers! Instead, pick the stocks that have high liquidity.

4. Trading based on gut instinct would work – around 10% of the time. The remaining 90% would cost you heavily! So, for consistent and steady profits, stick with your trading framework. Trust the numbers – they don't lie!

5. It is okay to wait it out if you do not find a good setup for entering trades. Desperation to trade just leads to losses.

6. The ideal amount of money to set aside for Penny Stock trading? $2000. Anything less would just lead to eating away your money before you even make profits.

7. Irrespective of the market conditions or direction, it is possible to make money as long as you have a good understanding of the basics.

8. The saying – don't put all your eggs in a single basket holds true for Penny Stocks as

well. Never invest all your money into a single stock.

9. Always be proactive in finding out any breaking news, product launches, or mergers. Sometimes, google alerts and Facebook discussions might shed light on new developments when analysts and news agencies cannot.

CONCLUSION

Thank you again for downloading this book!

I hope this book was able to help you to understand the advanced concepts, advanced analysis and advanced strategies for picking out Penny Stock winners.

The next step is to apply the strategies and techniques mentioned in the book in real life for becoming a successful professional trader in Penny Stocks.

Finally, if you enjoyed this book, then I'd like to ask you for a favor, would you be kind enough to leave a review for this book on Amazon? It'd be greatly appreciated!

Click here to leave a review for this book on Amazon!

Thank you and good luck!

CPSIA information can be obtained
at www.ICGtesting.com
Printed in the USA
BVHW04s1825140718
521642BV00021B/419/P